THE POISE GAME

Play to Become Your Best Self and to Live Your Best Life

Joseph Payton

THE POISE GAME

Play to Become Your Best Self and to Live Your Best Life

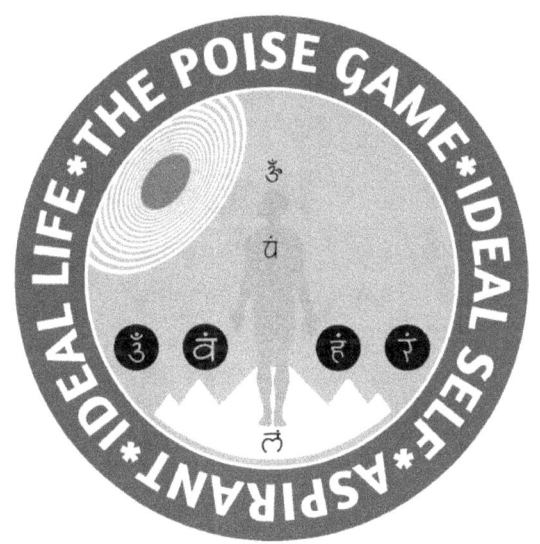

Joseph Payton

PAEGA LIFE
PUBLISHING

The characters and events depicted in this book are fictional. Any similarities to actual persons living or dead is purely coincidental.

Copyright © 2020 by Joseph Payton.

First Printing: December 2020

All rights reserved. Except as permitted by the U.S. Copyright Act of 1976, no part of this publication may be reproduced, distributed or transmitted in any form or by any means or stored in a database or retrieval system, without the prior written permission of the author or publisher.

Paega Life Publishing
Printed in the United States of America

ISBN-13: 978-1-7362620-1-6

Joseph Payton is available to speak at your organization, course or event on a variety of topics.

Email info@poisegame.com for booking information.

Visit us at www.PoiseGame.com

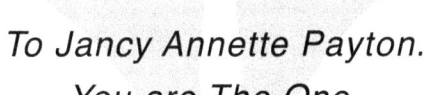

To Jancy Annette Payton.
You are The One.

To my children.
You are my legacy.

To my family and friends.
You sharpen me as iron sharpens iron.

Contents

	Prologue	1
1	Your Vision	5
2	Your Delusion	27
3	Your Game	45
4	Your Character	77
5	Your World	93
6	Your Tools	109
7	Your Team	139
8	Your Choice	155
9	Your Mindset	175
10	Your Priorities	197
11	Your Intentions	217
12	Your Beginning	233
13	Your Afterlife	251
	Epilogue	263
	The Poise Game Tools	267
	Glossary of Terms	279
	About the Author	290

Prologue

The sense that there is a purpose for you grows stronger. You've struggled to find clarity about it, and when you've tried to make any progress, your efforts seem futile.

But then you see a light. It glows red. It's like a beacon that summons you.

You begin to have glimpses of a vision. It seems to be you, but you're diffcrent. You seem to be content. Everything around you seems to be ideal.

You don't know why, but you believe your answers can be found wherever that light is located. If you could only find your way.

With what's left of your hope, you make a decision

that the prize is worth your effort. You're heading toward the light.

At the moment you make your choice, you stumble upon a book entitled, *The Poise Game*.

And as if the Divine was answering your call, you see that this book states that it can show you how to play to become your best self and to live your best life.

Inspired by this stroke of fortune, you choose to open the book to chapter one and begin to read.

Your Vision

"In that power of self-control lives the seed of eternal freedom."

Paramahansa Yogananda

You are an Aspirant.

"You can find infinite peace in your heart. You can have that life now," said the voice.

William was seven years old when he heard these encouraging words.

He was still dreaming when he awoke, finding himself still in his bedroom in the top bunk bed where he'd fallen asleep. He frequently dreamed, but something about this one was different. He tried to recall the first part of the message, but couldn't remember it.

He also couldn't remember if it was a person who spoke to him or if it was words that floated inside his head.

Maybe it was the voice of God. Or, perhaps, just a figment of his imagination.

In either case, the certainty and matter-of-factness in the tone and the words resonated with him.

Years later, William discovered that having "that life now" was challenging.

He was a teenager who struggled to find his place.

He performed well in most activities he attempted. In fact, his performance was often exceptional. He had acquaintances and friends with whom he could socialize. However, despite his relative successes and relationships, he still felt lost, out of place and out of control.

William's parents were devout practitioners of their religion. Because of that, he and his siblings regularly participated in the temple events that occurred throughout the week. One evening, he experienced an interesting interaction while attending a faith group meeting with his family.

This interaction served as a wake-up call for who he was and the life he could live.

The faith group hosted a woman who purported herself as a divine seer—a prophetess, she said.

She intrigued William with her presentation. He wasn't sure whether it was the theatrics of her delivery or the confidence in her energy. But he and everyone else seemed to be mesmerized by her message.

After the event concluded, William debated with the other teens about the merits of the speaker's claims, as she approached the group, with all eyes focused toward him.

Gazing as if she could see his soul, she said, "You have a special blessing upon your life. Mark my words, young man, you will help countless people in this life through your words and actions."

She reached toward him with both of her hands extended and he instinctively responded by taking them with both of his. She smiled at him, allowing the purest form of communication to transmit through the silence. She nodded her head and departed.

William's sister, who was standing next to him during the exchange, was the first to break the silence.

"What was that about?"

"I don't know," he responded.

But the truth is that he did.

As he returned home, the memory of his childhood

dream from six years prior resurfaced with clarity and purpose. He remembered everything the voice said to him, including the part that he'd previously forgotten.

"You are special because you are you. You are capable, and you are equipped. You just need to be willing and demonstrate it by each choice you make every moment of your life. If you have poise, then you can be your best self and you can live your best life. You can find infinite peace in your heart. You can have that life now."

William experienced internal conflict with the greatness that existed within versus feelings of doubt created by external factors.

Just like William, you may be experiencing some cognitive dissonance, which corrupts your mind and incapacitates your body. Fortunately, your spirit, which harbors the truth about you, remains incorrupt and free. It's from that truth that you may remember who you are and the life you can live; that is, if you have poise.

What is Poise?

Poise is the act of deliberately choosing your thoughts, emotions, words and deeds. It is the ability to recognize your existing habits when they are contrary to what you desire, and making a concerted effort to stop them and eventually change to be consistent with your vision.

The reason this book was written is because demonstrating poise to be your best self and live your best life is hard. We know poise can also be referred to as self-control, but most psychologists call it self-regulation. This topic continues to be an enigma to experts. Decades ago, a pair of research psychologists attempted to uncover why self-regulation often fails.

Their findings suggested that you can put self-regulation failures into two general categories: underregulation and misregulation. According to Roy Baumeister and Todd Heatherton, underregulation is the failure to exert self-control while misregulation is the counterproductive exertion of self-control.

The Poise Game is designed to address these factors that contribute to your disillusionment. When you apply the tools and methods presented to you in this book, you will discover that you're never really out of control—you're just out of alignment with your vision. By following this prescription, you can create who you are and the life you desire to live one poised choice at a time.

Poise can produce the ideal self because it is a virtue of virtues. There are many Aspirants who believe self-control is evidence of a holy spirit, the divine embodiment of excellence, living within you.

According to ancient writings, there are nine characteristics that indicate a person is virtuous.

They are love, joy, peace, patience, kindness, goodness, gentleness, faithfulness and self-control.

This book presents methods and tools to use self-control, or as we called it, poise, to develop the other virtues.

When your other virtues are developed, it is evidence that you have become your ideal self and live your ideal life because you are complete in your experience of the divine.

The Aspirant

This book is written for the Aspirant.

An Aspirant is a person who has ambitions to achieve his or her highest ideals.

So, if you're reading this, then you are an Aspirant and this book is written for you.

You desire to take control of yourself and your life. You acknowledge that you aren't who you hoped to become.

Your life is something less than what you had hoped. You are open to consider practical advice

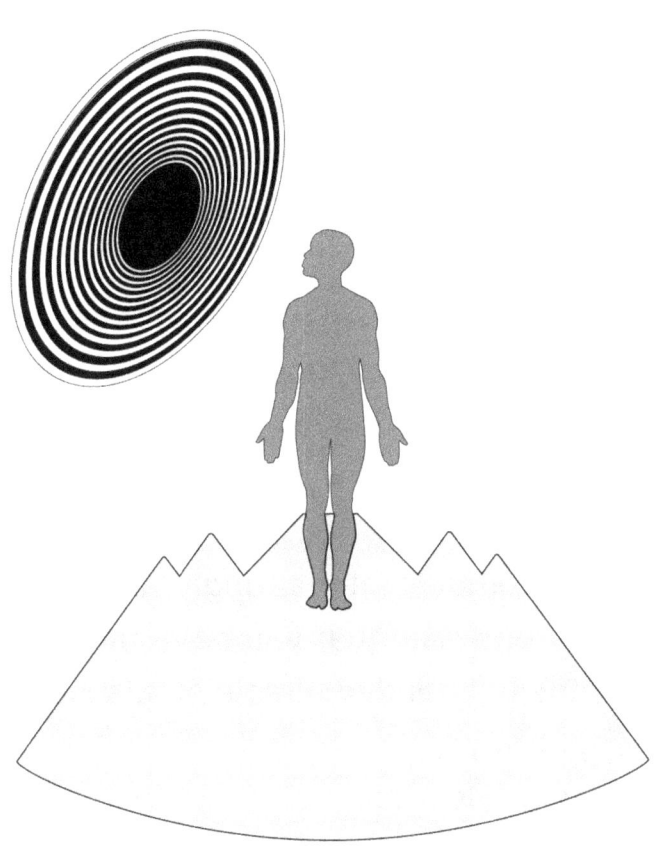

Poise Aspirant looking into the Apogee
that has the potential of helping you discover, make progress toward and achieve everything you ever dreamed.

You like to have fun and figure if you can become a better you and live a better life as the result of a game, then, "Why not give it a try?"

Visions are important because we experience our

perceptual reality via the form of pictures. These mental pictures represent what has happened, is happening and what is to come.

Our visions are especially important because they have the power to influence the quality of our lives.

There are times when we experience visions that depict undesirable circumstances. In certain psychotherapeutic modalities, it would be common practice for you to follow this vision down to its perceptual origin.

This is a method that I strongly advise against unless you are certain that you have the resilience to manage the unintended effects of this mental and emotional journey.

You should also ensure that your counselor, therapist, coach or guide is resilient because if he or she encounters triggers along your journey to the dark places of your being, then the result could be damaging to both of you.

Another way to address visions of undesirable circumstances is to consider what they are not.

By this I mean, what is the opposite vision?

My assumption is that if you're considering the opposite of an undesirable circumstance, then now you are envisioning a picture that is entirely desirable.

The mere fact that you can see it signifies something extremely important—that the desirable is real and it is possible.

In this case, visions are important because they are the launching pads from which you can reach your fullest potential.

The ideal self is the version of you that checks all your major marks regarding your aesthetics, attitudes, activities, affiliations and accomplishments.

When you are your ideal self, you are unabashed when entering an environment because your presence is exactly appropriate.

You intrinsically value yourself, and that is conveyed in all that you do and is clear to those with whom you engage.

You are honest about your intentions because your intentions are honest. You are free to choose that which brings you joy and are free to change your mind.

You are compassionate to everyone because you recognize that every person is on the journey to becoming him or herself, so in that we are all similar.

You acknowledge your past experiences, but emphasize your present events because you realize that they are all that exists.

You accept your emotional states for their utility and shift between them based upon their appropriateness for your priorities.

You are a victor of choice rather than a victim of circumstance. You are everything you aspire to be.

Your ideal life is the version of your life that checks all your major marks regarding atmosphere, domicile, topography, neighborhood, residence and climate.

When you are living your ideal life, you have desirable interpersonal engagements that respect your boundaries and the boundaries of others.

You are employed in occupations and vocations that allow you to demonstrate your best attributes, gifts and skills.

You participate in activities that inspire you and contribute to your joy. You reside in a location wherein the climate and terrain is conducive to your desires.

You lack nothing your heart desires because you know that it is already within your possession or it will arrive at the exact moment when you need it.

Benefits of this Book

This book is a motivational guide. It is a pragmatic handbook. It is a calibrated tool. It is a user's manual for your life. It is a reflecting pool showing you who you are and what you can do when you make a deliberate choice that prioritizes self-control, or in the case of this book, poise. The fruit that results from your poise is love—love of the divine, love of self and love of others.

This book will provide you with three useful items.

First and foremost, it will provide you an opportunity to be transparent with yourself in ways that you may have avoided due to your real and perceived obligations and the expectations you and others have developed for your persona. There is a special type of freedom—liberty—in being able to strip away the layers of armor and the calloused exterior that hides our truths. It's in this posture of your greatest vulnerabilities that you are most open and capable of tapping into your divine source of power—your self-control. Your poise. This book helps guide you into the posture that sets the proper conditions for the best version of you and the best possible life to become a reality.

Second, this book will provide you with a gamified format that can be used either as prescribed or modified to your preferences to help you make measurable progress toward achieving your desired outcomes. Oftentimes, you are your worst critic because you either give yourself way more credit than you deserve or you don't give yourself enough credit. These extreme forms of criticism lead to a life of depravity, if not in terms of accomplishments, then in terms of self-actualization and fulfillment. Using the methods described in this book, you will create constructive techniques for evaluating yourself and your life. You'll be able to acknowledge your intentions and your efforts based upon merit and outcomes.

Lastly, this book will assist you in creating a source of encouragement for you and others. By making progress through the readings and activities and by sharing with others what you are remembering, learning and experiencing, you will inevitably find yourself in a state of inspiration. The root word of inspiration is 'inspire.' The origin of this term relates to the act of taking air in. When you visualize a balloon that is empty or deflated, you can imagine an uninspired person. The uninspired person is one who hasn't experienced the benefit of his or her fullest potential. The moment a balloon begins to receive deposits of air, it takes its proper shape; it occupies the appropriate amount of space within its environment. Its fullest potential—its aesthetic and function—is realized. Why? Because it is literally inspired. That is what this book will do for you and those with whom you share it.

The Poise Game Snapshot

This book takes you on a journey beginning with 'Your Vision' in chapter one, which introduces you to the possibilities that you can have visions of your ideal self and life. The aim in chapter one is to set the conditions for you to begin demonstrating your self-control.

After seeing the ideal possibilities, you are reminded of 'Your Delusion' in chapter two. This chapter assists you with discovering the contributing factors to your impaired vision. Most importantly, it helps you to repair your vision when it's warped because your perspective is too small, full of blind spots or presenting obstacles rather than opportunities.

With the conditions established, chapter three shows you the rules of 'Your Game'—The Poise

Game. Here you will learn practical tools and methods designed to facilitate your self-control as you start, progress toward and attain your ideal self and ideal life.

Chapter four is part one of creating your vision board through your effort to identify who is 'Your Character'—the ideal self. Chapter five is part two of building your vision board by allowing you to establish 'Your World'—the ideal life. All of this is done beginning with your innermost vision and transitioning through all your senses to produce a tangible representation of what you desire to be and to experience.

It's one thing to see and otherwise sense your desires; it's another thing to deliberately chart a path toward bringing them to fruition. Chapter six, 'Your Tools,' shows you the tools to help you on your path. Via the Goals, Aspirations, and Initiatives Structure (GAInS), the Things to Do (T2D) list, the Efficient and Effective Activities (E2A), the Poise Deck, Powers, Triggers, and the Poise Aspirant Dashboard, you can lay out objective actions that lead you along the path to the person you choose to be and the life you choose to experience.

On the path to success, you will encounter

achievements as well as obstacles. That is why chapter seven will guide you through identifying 'Your Team' who will help you. Your Trusted Accountability Network, or TAN, will represent the people who celebrate with you during your joys, encourage you during your challenges and keep you accountable to your vision because these people have your best interests at heart.

If chapters four through seven were your tools, then chapters eight through 11 are your methods. Chapter eight shows you that you're capable of implementing 'Your Choice," which is the frame from which you perceive your experiences. You will learn to recognize that you can be a victor of choice versus victim of circumstance in all situations.

In chapter nine, you discover how to leverage your power of choice through 'Your Mindset.' You become aware that in order for you to be, do and have what you desire, you must wield your creative force through your thoughts, emotions, words and deeds.

With an understanding of your power, chapter 10 then presents a method that enables you to organize whatever is important to you according to 'Your Priorities." It is here where you recognize that those who prioritize don't compromise.

The final method is presented in chapter 11 as it helps you to identify with, and own, 'Your Intentions,' wherein you appreciate the value of taking actions that have good intentions without expectations of a specific result.

Finally, the book concludes in chapter 12 with a new start—'Your Beginning.' You've learned tools and methods of the game, so now you can start playing with clarity and purpose. You can begin your journey to become your best self and to live your best life, now.

You might be confused that I stated the book concludes with chapter 12, when there are clearly 13 chapters according to the table of contents. Here's the deal. If you read chapters one through 12, as an Aspirant you will have everything you need in terms of tools and methods to be your best self and live your best life in terms of the natural order of things. But the benefit of your efforts stop when you die. Chapter 13 is for you if you have ever considered the possibility of 'Your Afterlife.' You don't need to read it to benefit from the rest of the book, but ask yourself: "Why would I want to gain the world and lose my soul?" Read chapter 13 and maybe you'll discover you can be your best self and live your best life, now and forever.

How to Read this Book

The beauty of this book is that it can be read in any way you prefer. Each chapter delivers sufficient information that will provide value to you. Period. But, if you want to know how I would read this book, then let me tell you. I would start where you are currently, with chapter one so you get an understanding of what is coming in the subsequent chapters. Then, I would complete the book in the following chapter order: 3, 6-11, 4-5, and then 2, 12, and finally 13.

You are probably wondering why I didn't publish the book in this order to save you from the mental gymnastics.

That's a fair question.

The reason the book is published in its current order is because this order is most logical if you plan on reading and completing the exercises straight through. Admittedly, chapters four and five may delay progress as you overcome mental obstacles that hinder the clear picture of your idealized self and life. For that reason, I recommend skipping them for anyone who would find that exercise discouraging.

Once you've learned the structure and methods for realizing your desires, which are outlined in succession in the prescribed reading order, then you will be empowered to explore your full potential and imagine the best version of yourself and your life that previously seemed to be unattainable and beyond your wildest dreams.

This book is special because even if you: (1) believe it's possible to be your ideal self and live your ideal life, (2) create your tools, and (3) adhere to the methods, then you will experience deliberate joy, satisfaction and contentment in this life.

How many books have you read that promise you that you can design yourself and the life you desire in three simple steps? That's a rhetorical question, but my guess is that if you're reading this book, then the others didn't work—at least not for you.

Games are Fun

This book is called *The Poise Game* because I discovered a long time ago that the greatest minds were right—life sucks! That is, if you take it too seriously and don't become the person or live the life of which you can be proud. I've traveled to several countries around the world, and one thing I notice is that people, despite ethnicity, socio-economic status, gender or age, seek opportunities to have fun. There's nothing more fun than playing games, and we all have an innate knack for creating the most fun games in creative and imaginable ways using the least interesting resources and seemingly daunting circumstances.

So, why do most of us agree that life sucks? Well, it's because it's no fun. And it is the least fun when two things are prevalent: (1) you have a lack of control, and (2) you have an abundance of work. But there is another problem. There are only a few things you can literally control. And you must work—if not for sustainment, then for sanity. So, what does all of this have to do with The Poise Game?

Though there are many things you can't control, one of the things you can control is yourself.

You saw that coming, didn't you?

If someone were to observe you demonstrate self-control, how do you think that person would describe you in one word that starts with the letter "P" and ends with "Oised"?

Poised. Yes.

And since it's more fun to play games than it is

to work, I decided to make The Poise Game, where you win each time you demonstrate poise.

Now life can suck a lot less because life never sucks when you're winning.

This book shows you how.

Your Delusion

"Respect the delicate ecology of your delusions."

Tony Kushner

Are you delusional?

Frankly, most of us are. Especially when we're trying to make sense of everything that appears to be happening to us. And that, my friend, is the real delusion. When you perceive your experience as if you're the butt at the end of the universe's sadistic joke, then this is an indicator that your vision is impaired.

Impaired vision is a picture that misrepresents you and your life. When what you see is contrary to what you desire, then you have two options.

One, you can accept it as your fundamental reality and plunge deeper into the darkness that destroys hope by rendering you blind.

Or two, you can acknowledge it as a symptom of your perceptual reality and ascend higher toward the light that amplifies your faith by bringing clarity to your vision.

Impaired vision is dangerous because, despite its negative effects, your vision—good, bad and inconsequential—belongs to you.

The dangers relating to impaired vision cause risks to your health, wealth, relationships and happiness. When you don't see an accurate picture, then your thoughts, emotions, words and deeds all become questionable.

With regards to matters of your physical fitness, mental fitness and overall wellness, what should you do?

Are you in need of drastic measures to make improvements to these areas or should you continue what you're already doing?

What about the things that contribute to your wealth, like your employment, investments, businesses and property?

Are you in the right industry for you based upon your life's purpose?

Are you sufficiently compensated to meet your needs and the needs of the people and the causes you care about?

Then there's your relationships.

Do the people you love know it?

Does an assessment of your time demonstrate the value you've assigned to your friends and loved ones?

How about your countenance?

Are you sure things are as bad as they appear?

When you experience joy, is it superficial or does it come from a deeper place?

What makes you so sure?

Impaired vision causes you to question your own sensibilities. If you can't be sure about the accuracy of your own perceptions, the logical conclusion is that you can't be sure about anything.

If you can't trust your own senses about anything, then you can't trust yourself. And if you can't trust yourself, then who or what can you trust?

Just thinking about it can stir up emotions and anxiety. This is the danger of impaired vision. This is what it causes.

Causes of Impaired Vision

The degradation of your vision can be attributed to several causes. There is an exhaustive and debatable list of malignant factors, but for the sake of understanding how your vision becomes impaired, we'll discuss the causes that I believe you can directly address and, consequently, you can fix.

The first cause of impaired vision is pain. Pain can occur at any time and be experienced physically and emotionally. I'm sure you're aware that understanding pain can be tricky because sometimes things that appear catastrophic cause minimal pain, while things that appear inconsequential cause pain that is unbearable.

The second cause is shame. Think about a time when you were ashamed. Perhaps you're feeling that way right now. The weight, the pressure, the burden of it all compresses your lungs and constricts your airways. You can't breathe. It's as if some malevolent force has you by the throat and with an evil grin watches you gasp in a labored effort to take your next breath.

The third cause of vision impairment is denial. Denial occurs in a couple ways. One way it occurs is when you don't believe you deserve anything positive. The other way denial occurs is more deceptive. What's strange about it is that you think others are obstructing your access to things, experiences and feelings you desire. However, when you look behind the curtain, you discover a familiar face is the puppet master manipulating the strings of the marionette. That familiar face is you. Although you can identify the face, you refuse to acknowledge that you are both the puppeteer and the puppet.

The fourth cause is pessimism. This occurs when you have personally experienced hardships or observed undesirable circumstances in the lives of others, and can't muster the resolve to believe that eventually the sun will shine through the rain clouds. When you have lost all hope, and begin to believe that good outcomes are no longer possible, then pessimism has taken over.

The benefit of knowing the four causes of impaired vision is that you can learn to identify their associated indicators. When your vision is impaired, it's almost like you're absent of all your useful faculties. Your five senses plus your intuition, which I believe is the sixth sense, are unreliable. In this state, you must depend upon the primal substance that exists within you that is designed to survive. It combats all things that seek to destroy it. When you take the time to still your mind, it will highlight the indicators of your impaired vision.

I've shown you how each of these causes can arise, but what is it about them that impairs your vision?

What do these causes of impaired vision have in common?

Fear is the Foundation of Your Delusion

The common denominator is fear.

The above causes of your impaired vision—pain, shame, denial and pessimism—each are representations of your deepest fears.

Pain represents your fear of being hurt.

Shame represents your fear of being rejected.

Denial represents your fear of being wrong.

Pessimism represents your fear of losing someone who, or something that, matters the most to you.

The verdict is out—when you experience fear, that is the indicator that your vision is impaired.

If you're wondering why it matters if your vision is impaired or not, then let's look at its impact.

When you are delusional, which is the result of impaired vision, your thoughts, emotions, words and deeds will be insufficient and misguided because they are based upon inaccurate information.

For example, let's say you desire to travel to an

exotic destination. Imagine that place. If it were me, I'd pick Costa Rica. If you can't think of anywhere, then you can use Costa Rica, too.

Now, let's say you aren't sure where you currently are? Assuming in this scenario that you couldn't rely on a GPS or Internet-based location service to give you accurate information regarding your location, could you reasonably begin making your way to Costa Rica?

The answer is no.

Your lack of clarity—your impaired vision—impacted your efforts to achieve your desired results. In fact, when your vision is impaired, it's possible for your well-intended efforts to move you further from your desired outcomes because they are based upon misperception.

The fears that obscure and distort your perspective can act as dangerous instigators for behaviors that, under other circumstances, may be warranted.

Impaired vision misrepresents each situation and raises the risks associated with everything you do. In doing so, it inhibits your progress to becoming your ideal self and living your ideal life.

Recognizing the indicators of impaired vision

are essential for mitigating their effects and, consequently, restoring and maintaining clear vision.

Status of Your Vision

You are likely in one of a few situations. You are either transitioning from clear vision to impaired vision, maintaining your impaired vision,

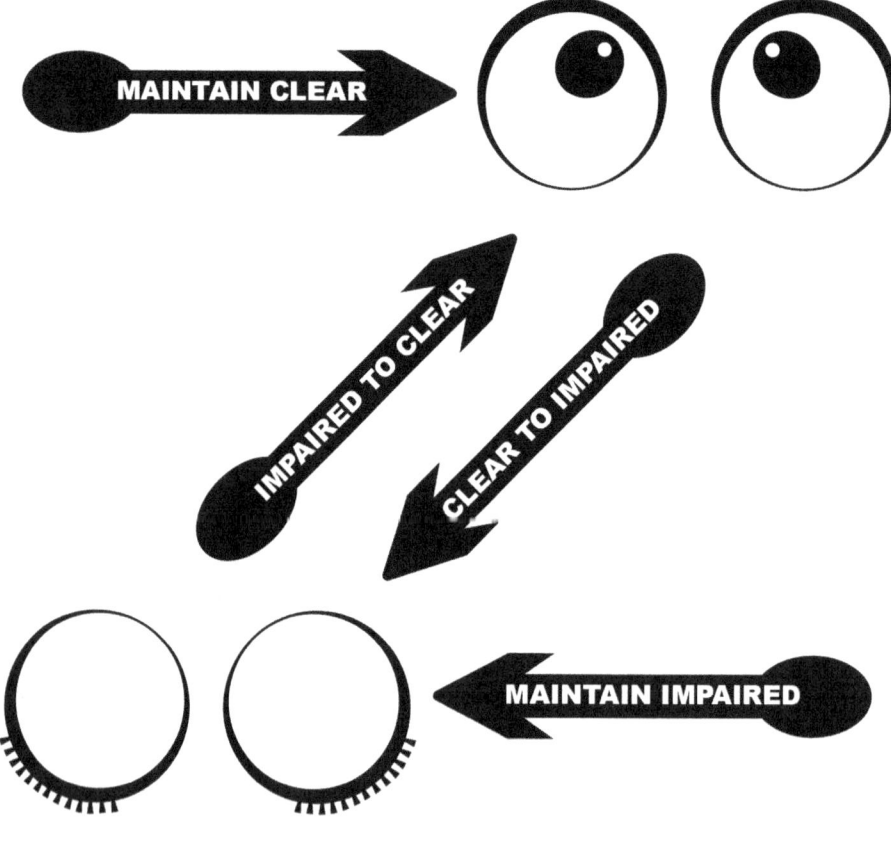

Vision Continuum

transitioning from impaired vision to clear vision, or maintaining clear vision.

If you're transitioning from clear vision to impaired vision or doing your best to maintain your impaired vision, then you can stop. Right now as you read, you are receiving the antidote to the venomous snake bite that degrades your true picture of yourself and your possibilities. If you're in the thick of your delusion, your vision is impaired and that is your status quo. You can take the first step by acknowledging that although the feelings you're experiencing are real, the perceptions can change if you change them. You have that ability when your vision is clear.

If you're transitioning from impaired vision to clear vision, be mindful that you remain vigilant against the familiarity of your former delusions. That familiarity disguises itself in a sheepskin of comfort, but is a ravaging wolf capable of wreaking havoc on your hopeful opportunities.

If you're maintaining your clear vision, then you are a special person who has the time and capacity to move toward becoming your ideal self and living your ideal life. You can help others out of their delusions, but be mindful because the further you progress, the more humility you'll need to develop.

Humility will act as your security measure for the subtle events that attack your truths about yourself and your life. If your humility doesn't match or exceed your success, then you are at a risk for a catastrophic event that could damage your vision and make it difficult for you to disbelieve what you see as a result of fear because you've come to trust in your vision for so long.

No matter what category you may fall into, it is important to know the indicators of impaired vision to mitigate its negative effects.

The truth is that we're all susceptible to having impaired vision. But the good news is that we're all inclined to have clear vision as well.

Metacognition is Thinking about Thinking

You know how to describe impaired vision, what its causes are, what its indicators are and why it's important for you to know this information, even if your vision is clear. Now we'll look at how to overcome it and inoculate ourselves against it. Regardless if you're in the prison of your delusion or if you're in the freedom of your clarity, you must rely upon your inborn safety device—metacognition. Metacognition, Greek for "after" (meta) and "thought" (cognition), refers to the human capacity to be aware of and control one's own thoughts and internal mental processes.

You may not know it by this name, but it's something you do frequently and mostly involuntarily.

You do it when you're happy. You do it when you're sad. You do it when you're among others. You do it when you're alone.

Metacognition is thinking about thinking, and you do it all the time. The way to leverage this natural ability to restore and maintain your clear vision is to deliberately audit your thoughts. While metacognition can occur involuntarily, you must employ it with intention. You must become an intelligence analyst who is mining the data trails for anomalies and patterns. You must learn which ones perpetuate obscurity and which ones proliferate clarity. As you refine this natural talent into a skill, you will learn to implement it on a schedule to periodically perform maintenance upon your vision.

Similar to the periodic checks and services that a mechanic performs on your car to ensure it continues to operate optimally, you'll do the same for your vision. When you follow the prescribed service schedule on your car, you mitigate potential functional damages that could, if not addressed early, be extremely costly, or worse, dangerous. This applies to the practice of deliberate metacognition where you assess the quantity and quality of your thoughts in relation to your ideal self and ideal life. If they do not contribute toward your progress, then they need to be adjusted, fixed, or abandoned.

We will discuss ways to implement metacognition later in chapter eight. There you'll learn that your thoughts are just one of the four aspects of the source of your power to become the person and live the life you choose.

If you desire to dig deeper into that subject now, then you can jump ahead and return here later. Just mark your spot. If not, then let's continue. Either way, it's your choice.

A Strong Offense Against Impaired Vision

Now that you're well-versed in the implications of impaired vision, let's shift our energies in a positive direction.

Although this chapter seems to clearly focus on exposing, explaining and eradicating your impaired vision, that's not the point.

I've spent this time describing the dangers of delusions to teach you the fundamentals of a proper defense. But anyone who has ever faced an adversary will tell you that the best defense is a strong offense.

Your strong offense is your clear vision. The fact that clarity is supreme when it comes to vision sounds obvious.

For instance, just imagine you're looking through a window and observing whatever objects comprise the scenery.

If you're near a window go ahead and do this now. When the window is clean and fully transparent, you can experience the landscape as it truly exists. However, as the window becomes dirty and the filth begins to spread across the surface, it's no longer transparent. It's now translucent and your view is distorted. If nothing is done to address the grime, eventually the window becomes opaque, and your vision is completely obstructed and impaired.

Clear vision allows you to recognize and appreciate your truths. If impaired vision means you meander through the darkness, then clear vision means you stride through the light.

With clarity, fear does not exist because fear is a byproduct of uncertainty.

Clear vision enables your certainty and,

therefore, it engenders the confidence that you have value and your aspirations are not arbitrary goals; rather, they are the adventures that lead to the ideal representation of who you are and the life you choose to live.

Clear vision is important because it sets the proper conditions for your thoughts, emotions, words and deeds so that they contribute toward you achieving your desired outcomes. In these conditions you are able to extend and expand vision across the other senses, thus mobilizing the entire capacity of your abilities.

Vision Includes All Your Senses

I'm going to take a guess that if I were to ask you, "Which sense do you connect with vision?" your immediate answer would be "sight."

While that makes sense, the reality is that vision comprises all our senses in varying degrees to form a collective conceptual experience.

The more senses that participate, the more real the experience. Interestingly, for decades performance psychologists have applied visualization techniques for everyone from athletes to soldiers, and even to abuse victims to help them create resonant personal experiences that they can use to better perform given they find themselves in or dealing with those situations that were simulated.

During these simulations, brain scans show that the areas of the brain that relate to the simulated activities are engaged. They light up with activity. This means that conceptually the brain experienced the situation as if it really occurred.

So it's through the portal of your vision that you are able to engage your other senses of touch, taste, smell and hearing to actively rehearse your chosen experiences.

In that way, you don't need to follow the old adage: "fake it 'til you make it." You take that adage and remix it: "visualize it 'til you realize it."

All this talk about vision can't be glossed over as a formality.

You're reading this book, so I'm assuming you're interested in becoming your best self and living your best life. If that's the case, then it is vitally important that you spend time developing your natural talent of metacognition into a bona fide skill.

At a minimum, you should know where you stand in terms of your vision.

Are you on a damaging down-spiral transitioning from clear vision to impaired vision?

Are you settling for a delusional status quo of maintaining your impaired vision?

Or are you following the light out of the tunnel by transitioning from impaired vision to clear vision?

Can you already see clearly and are maintaining your clear vision?

Your vision status will assist you with making the productive decisions that advance you.

Knowing your vision status is essential to playing The Poise Game, which is designed to help you implement tools and methods to become your ideal self and live your ideal life.

Speaking of the game, how about I explain it to you and show you how to play it?

Your Game

"Remember that poise and power are inseparably associated. The calm and balanced mind is the strong and great mind; the hurried and agitated mind is the weak one."

Wallace D. Wattles

The Poise Game is more than a game.

As an Aspirant on your journey to discover your highest ideals, it's your guide. It's your way of life. It's the device you use to channel and optimize your power in the most productive way possible.

By playing this game, you demonstrate your power to choose to become your ideal self and live your ideal life.

There's no gimmick. It takes effort to combat the plethora of contrarian stimuli and disruptive ideas that breed dread, doubt and despair. And since your brain is more amenable to recreation rather than vocation, I've created The Poise Game to transform your most important work you'll do in life into play.

If I were to compare the gameplay experience to anything, then The Poise Game is your real-life first-person shooter, action, adventure, sports, fighting, simulation, strategy and role-playing game all wrapped into one.

Like in any other game, you must select your character. In this case, selecting the character is easy because it's you.

It is technically a one-player game, but I've found the experience adds a different aspect of excitement when played in concert with others.

During the game, you establish goals, aspirations and initiatives that lead to your predetermined vision.

Your vision consists of two parts—the idealized version of yourself and the idealized version of your life.

Is it Possible to Achieve Your Dreams?

What if it is possible for you to become your ideal self? How about if it were possible to live your ideal life? What if you can achieve them both and help others do so, too?

I believed the answers to those were questions I

had were somewhere out there.

You've heard stories about people going from abject to affluent, rags to riches, pauper to prince. Typically, their anecdotes are shared with the masses after they're well into their fame.

That's not my story.

My wealth is emergent.

And while I could follow the status quo and wait until I've fully attained paradise, that's not my modus operandi.

From my observations and experiences, I've pieced together a format—a game—that helps you achieve your wildest dreams. And I'm sharing it with you now so we can take this journey together.

I've spent most of my adult life trying to grasp the keys to a fulfilling life.

There were times when I felt glimpses of the elusive prize; yet, it seldom remained long enough for me to wallow in it.

At one point I began to despair, concluding that despite the tangible beauty, success, and abundance in my life, discontentment was my plight.

Initially, my hope for obtaining contentment was based upon the holy books, the prophets, the sages, and the gurus that have taught about its attainment.

Then I began to notice something.

I was seeing people who possess contentment in their lives.

Each person is different, but they all embody one characteristic—they unapologetically make deliberate productive decisions to make progress toward their vision.

This book is my tribute to those people whose examples inspired me to create this systematic approach in the form of a game to strive to have a fulfilling life.

The Poise Game Fundamentals

The gameplay for The Poise Game follows the graduated poise pattern, which includes these five steps: (1) Review, (2) Assess, (3) Refine, (4) Focus, and (5) Choose.

I recommend applying the steps in stage order, especially when you are first beginning, because this will help you train and develop your poise instincts.

However, you can choose to go to a specific stage, especially if the situation demands it. Or you can play at any stage based upon your preference.

Remember, this game is entirely about you recognizing the power of choice and accepting responsibility for its results whether good, bad, or inconsequential.

Poise is demonstrated by deliberate and effectual thoughts, emotions, words and deeds.

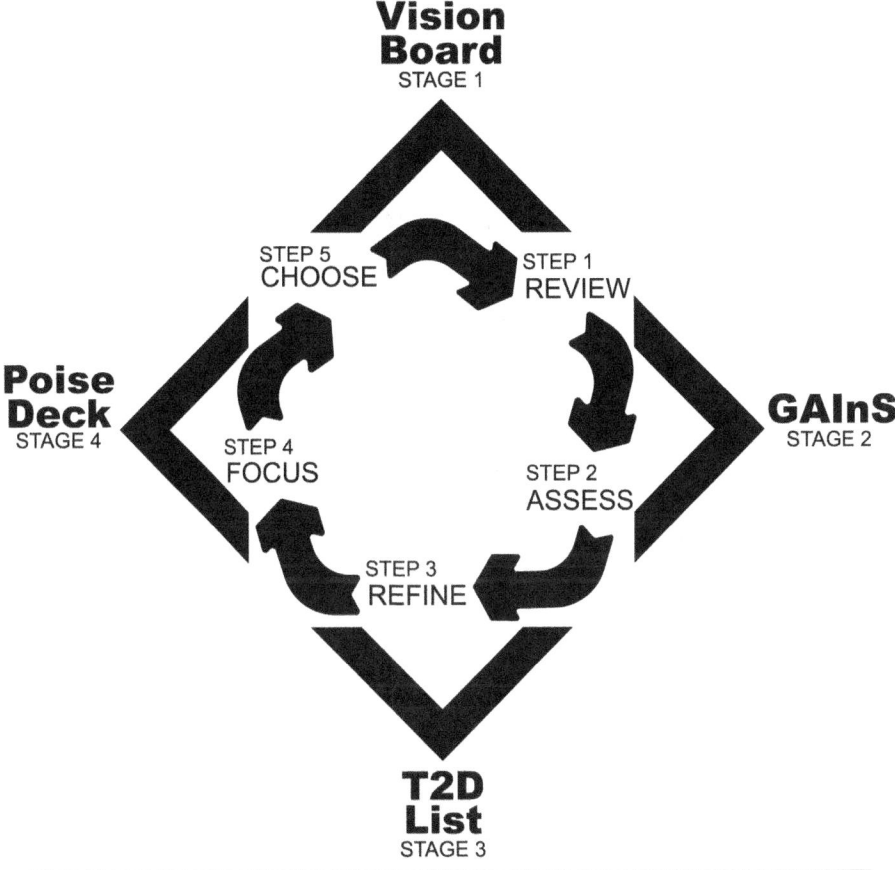

Poise Game Stages & Graduated Poise Pattern Steps

There are four stages where you can apply the graduated poise pattern. These stages are aptly named for The Poise Game tool used to play them.

In stage one, Vision Board, you consider what you've chosen as the final destination on your vision board—your end game. It's depicted in the way that most resonates with you to ensure it serves as both a motivator and an accountability device when encountered. At this level, you can choose to complete a custom efficient and effective activity (E2A) or select a generic one from your E2A List that contributes to the progress toward any aspect of your Vision Board. Make sure to record the count of each E2A you complete on your Poise Aspirant Dashboard. Also, annotate on your Poise Aspirant Dashboard any completed GAInS Adventures.

In stage two, GAInS, you consider what you've chosen as your adventures for the current year on your Goals, Aspirations, and Initiatives Structure (GAInS). These items should connect to the larger vision and may take some time to accomplish. That is why they are reset on an annual basis. You can either select a GAInS Adventure or you can roll the d-8 (an eight-sided dice corresponding to the eight GAInS Adventure categories, including 1-physical, 2-recreational, 3-vocational, 4-relational, 5-financial, 6-educational, 7-mental and 8-spiritual) to reduce your selection options to a specific GAInS Adventure category from which you can choose. Each number on the dice corresponds with the number for the GAInS Adventure category. You can play without the dice, but it adds an interesting aspect when you're looking to add some excitement to your choices. Choose to complete a custom E2A or select a generic one from your E2A List that contributes to the progress toward the selected GAInS Adventure. Make sure to record the count of each of the E2As you complete on your Poise Aspirant Dashboard, and annotate on your Poise Aspirant Dashboard any completed GAInS Adventures, if applicable.

In stage three, T2D, you consider the Things to Do (T2D) List for any daily, weekly, monthly, or quarterly tasks that you must accomplish to make progress toward your GAInS and, thus, your Vision Board. Sometimes they can take on a flavor of the mundane because you may have responsibilities that do not appear to directly relate to your Vision. The key to T2D items is your ability to prioritize and apply your power of choice. Ideally, the actions directly contribute to your adventures, but if they don't, then ensure, at a minimum, you are benefiting from the act of making a deliberate choice, which is the foundational component of poise. Complete the custom E2As and generic E2As on your T2D List. Record the count of each of the E2As you complete on your Poise Aspirant Dashboard, and annotate on your Poise Aspirant Dashboard any completed GAInS Adventures, if applicable.

In stage four, Poise Deck, you consider the E2As you selected to comprise your deck and give yourself an opportunity to choose based upon the shuffling and selection of a card and several cards, depending on how much you prefer to play. This level can be used as a fun way to practice developing your poise. It can also be used as your fail-safe when you find yourself idle, feeling incapacitated, feeling uninspired, or feeling depressed.

To play the Poise Deck:

1. Shuffle the deck.

2. Draw the top card and read the prompt.

3. If you draw an E2A, then either choose to complete the E2A or choose to return the card to the bottom of the deck.

4. If you choose to return the card to the bottom of the deck, then draw another card.

5. If you draw a 'Do whatever you want' card, then either choose a custom E2A or select a

generic E2A from the Poise Deck to complete.

6. Continue this pattern until you select a card that leads to you choosing to complete an E2A.

7. Repeat as many times as you prefer.

Record the count of each of the E2As you complete on your Poise Aspirant Dashboard, and annotate on your Poise Aspirant Dashboard any completed GAInS Adventures, if applicable.

The Poise Game Scoring & Level-up Criteria

It's important to make this disclaimer: you can play The Poise Game without focusing on advancing through the levels described below.

The utility of applying its tools and methods will still positively impact your experience, regardless if you track your level and points. That said, there is a benefit to keeping a tally on your successes. Particularly in times when you're not feeling motivated or you're feeling as if you haven't accomplished anything, your completed GAInS, GAInS Adventures, T2D Lists, and E2As will be factual proof to the contrary.

That said, you can skip the rest of this paragraph if you don't care about the scoring and level-up

LEVEL	GAInS Adventures	E2As
01	12	360
02	24	720
03	36	1080
04	48	1440
05	60	1800
06	60	1500
07	48	1200
08	36	900
09	24	600
10	12	360
11	16	730
12	24	1095
13	32	1460
14	24	1095
15	16	730
16	8	730
17	8	1095
18	8	1460
19	8	1825
20	8	365

*Completing an annual GAInS equals automatic level-up

The Poise Game Level-up Chart

requirements. Or you can read the rest of it just in case you decide to keep track of them later.

Everyone who begins the game starts as a Level Zero Aspirant.

The way to advance to the next level is to complete an annual GAInS, complete the requisite amount of GAInS Adventures for each level, or complete the requisite amount of E2As for each level.

Completed E2As are captured using the T2D List and Poise Deck. Completing an annual GAInS is an automatic level up. The values of GAInS Adventures and E2A point requirements adjust as you progress in level.

Each completed GAInS Adventure equals an Adventure point. Each E2A completed equals an E2A point. You can level up at any time you reach level-up requirements.

You must exchange the respective points for the next level, which returns your score to zero in the point categories that you've exchanged.

Here is The Poise Game level-up criteria through level 20:

Level 01. Complete the Annual GAInS or 12 GAInS Adventures or 360 E2As.

Level 02. Complete the Annual GAInS or 24 GAInS Adventures or 720 E2As.

Level 03. Complete the Annual GAInS or 36 GAInS Adventures or 1080 E2As.

Level 04. Complete the Annual GAInS or 48 GAInS Adventures or 1440 E2As.

Level 05. Complete the Annual GAInS or 60 GAInS Adventures or 1800 E2As.

Level 06. Complete the Annual GAInS or 60 GAInS Adventures or 1500 E2As.

Level 07. Complete the Annual GAInS or 48 GAInS Adventures or 1200 E2As.

Level 08. Complete the Annual GAInS or 36 GAInS Adventures or 900 E2As.

Level 09. Complete the Annual GAInS or 24 GAInS Adventures or 600 E2As.

Level 10. Complete the Annual GAInS or 12 GAInS Adventures or 360 E2As.

Level 11. Complete the Annual GAInS or 16 GAInS Adventures or 730 E2As.

Level 12. Complete the Annual GAInS or 24 GAInS Adventures or 1095 E2As.

Level 13. Complete the Annual GAInS or 32 GAInS Adventures or 1460 E2As.

Level 14. Complete the Annual GAInS or 24 GAInS Adventures or 1095 E2As.

Level 15. Complete the Annual GAInS or 16 GAInS Adventures or 730 E2As.

Level 16. Complete the Annual GAInS or 8 GAInS Adventures or 730 E2As.

Level 17. Complete the Annual GAInS or 8 GAInS Adventures or 1095 E2As.

Level 18. Complete the Annual GAInS or 8 GAInS Adventures or 1460 E2As.

Level 19. Complete the Annual GAInS or 8 GAInS Adventures or 1825 E2As.

Level 20. Complete the Annual GAInS or 8 GAInS Adventures or 365 E2As.

Another item that is tracked in The Poise Game is Vision Points.

These are earned when you as the Aspirant achieve one of the images reflected in your Vision Board. Vision points don't advance you in level, but they add a modifier on your Poise Level showing that you have not only been diligent in demonstrating poise, as reflected by your level, but you are also progressing toward your vision.

Once you hit level 20, you will have had a minimum of 20 completed GAInSs or 512 completed GAInS Adventures or 20,245 completed E2As.

Any combination of these deliberate choices over the course of 20 years, assuming they were connected to your vision of your ideal self and ideal life, would have developed within you the habit of demonstrating poise.

If you haven't realized the images of your ideal self and life by level 20, then I suspect you're well on your way and have the tools, methods and support necessary to reach your desired outcomes.

You can continue to play the game and track your statistics as a level 20, which would likely bring another type of excitement, especially if you've been playing the game with members of your TAN.

Preparing to Play the Game

This game is designed to be an experience of winning from the moment you choose to create your tools through the completion of each E2A to the point when you realize the person and life depicted on your Vision Board is what you are currently experiencing.

You're going to need to collect some items before you're ready to play the game. Some of them may already be in your house. Some you may need to purchase. Most of them, if you think creatively, can be gathered by repurposing stuff that may be intended for other uses.

The resources prescribed are what you need to make the analog tools that support the physical game-play experience in the quickest and most economical way.

They include:

- Standard 52-card deck
- Card deck carrier
- d8 or 8-sided dice

- Package of at least 52 labels with adhesive
- Permanent marker
- Pocket, wall or desk calendar
- Notepad
- Pen and pencil
- Poster board
- Scissors
- Tape or glue
- Magazine or newspapers (ones you're okay with damaging)

Don't let these items limit or inhibit your ability to play the game. If you feel you can automate a portion or all aspects, then do it.

This is The Poise Game; but more importantly, it's your game.

No one can win for you, so if you adjust certain aspects to your preference, then you're operating in the spirit of this game's purpose. Things that make you uniquely you include your DNA, your fingerprints and your soul. I fully expect your version of The Poise Game to also be uniquely you. You can and should tailor it to suit your needs. And you know if it works because it works for you.

Once you have the resources, you can work on

preparing your tools. You'll use the items above to create the tools that you'll need to play the game. These tools will require investments from you of your time and your thoughts. This step can occur quickly if you have a good idea of your vision and the steps it takes to achieve it, or it can take some time as you contemplate and work to discover your vision and the adventures that bring it into fruition.

The Poise Game Tools Overview

You'll need to think practically about what you believe is the ideal situation for you.

And given that situation, what are your convictions and goals, how do you prefer to characterize them, and who do you trust to help you achieve them?

Later chapters are dedicated to detailing why these tools are important, how to build and tailor them to your needs, and recommendations about when and how to employ them best.

Here is the list of The Poise Game tools you'll need to create with brief descriptions.

The Vision Board presents your ideal self and ideal life. It's important that it is physically represented because it forces you to translate your concept into something that exists beyond your mind. This is an essential step to transform your dreams into your reality.

The Personal Mission Statement (PMS) is a short paragraph, at least two sentences, that highlight your intrinsic mandate for yourself. It's your marching orders. It gives you an understanding of the spirit of your vision so in the absence of any specific objectives or tasks, if your thoughts, emotions, words and deeds reflect your mission statement, then they are contributing to your progress.

The Personal Conviction Mantra (PCM) is a short declaration that helps remind you of your mission and your vision. It can be one word or an entire sentence. It serves to motivate, correct, honor, and support thoughts, emotions, words and deeds that lead to the demonstration of poise.

The Goals, Aspirations, and Initiatives Structure (GAInS) organizes predetermined annual adventures into one of eight categories:

1. Physical
2. Recreational
3. Vocational
4. Relational
5. Financial
6. Educational
7. Mental

8. Spiritual.

The GAInS helps you to make a choice regarding what's important and to be accountable and aware of areas that may lack balance because you have chosen to emphasize some and disregard others. In each category, the objectives you intend to complete are called GAInS Adventures.

The Things to Do List, or T2D List, represents a selection of tasks that support the annual adventures listed in the GAInS. The T2D List comprises daily, weekly, monthly, or quarterly tasks. This depends and varies based upon your preference and the amount of time you want to spend applying the graduated poise pattern to this level.

The Efficient and Effective Activities, or E2As, are the individual tasks that are the building blocks to completing your T2D List, accomplishing your GAInS, and reaching your Vision. They may be found on your T2D List and are the heart of your Poise Deck.

The Poise Deck consists of as many cards as you prefer. I recommend keeping it simple and sticking with a traditional 52-playing card deck. On the face side of each card contains an E2A. Chapter 6 will describe the Poise Deck in more detail, but you can think of it as your Swiss Army Knife for poise. You can use it in several different contexts because it represents the bare bones of what The Poise Game is all about—giving you the opportunity to make deliberate and productive choices.

The Trusted Accountability Network (TAN) is a critical component to supporting you on your journey to becoming your best self and living your best life. It's composed of the important people you know who are honest, insightful, trustworthy, industrious and, most importantly, have your best interests at heart.

The Powers represent your notable skills, talents, qualities and attributes. These are things that you will use and leverage along your journey. You will aim to maintain or develop them more thoroughly as you achieve your adventures.

The Triggers represent the sensitive areas and topics that can cause you to respond instinctively in an unproductive way. The reason they are not described as weaknesses is because their purpose is designed to focus on protecting you now. We want to know them so we can develop a secondary trigger release that allows you to know when the response to the trigger will be productive or counterproductive.

The Poise Aspirant Dashboard can be thought of as your own quick reference display. It will comprise many of the items listed above and orient them in a single place for quick reference. This will assist you when you want to reflect upon your vision, review it for relevance, or take account of your accomplished adventures and those yet to be achieved.

Setting up the Game

My father once told me that you can do anything as long as you have an effective method and you have the right tools. Gathering and creating the tangible and conceptual pieces to The Poise Game cannot be overlooked because they form critical components of what will make this game personally useful for you.

To set-up for playing The Poise Game is very easy, especially once you've created your tools.

Frankly, you can begin gameplay as soon as you know your vision and have established some GAInS and E2As. To play, select a GAInS, then pick an E2A that supports it, and do it.

That's an immediate victory.

Do it again, as often as you can, and you will continue to be a winner.

Eight-sided Dice (d8)

Those micro-wins will lead to the accomplishment of your adventures and eventually allow you to reach your vision.

If you'd like to take the time to play the game in a more systematic way, then you'll need to prepare all the tools described above.

Once you have them complete, then you'll take your Poise Aspirant Dashboard and begin with stage one and apply the graduated poise pattern.

At each stage, you can choose to do an E2A. After completing it, you can do it again or do something else.

The game is continuously going, so everything you do can impact the environment and perceived challenges and opportunities; but as an Aspirant that's okay because you're making deliberate choices that are in your best interests.

There are two quick ways to set-up the game.

First is to take the GAInS and the d-8. Roll the d-8, and whichever number you land on will correspond to one of the eight adventurer categories reflected on the GAInS. Roll the d-8 again until you land on the number of one of the GAInS Adventures listed in the selected category. Then, select an E2A that corresponds with that item.

The second, and probably the quickest way to play the game is possible once you've created your Poise Deck. You can shuffle the deck and pull a card depicting an E2A. Then, you either choose to do it or not. If you choose not to do it, place it at the bottom of the deck. If you choose to do it, then separate it from the deck to keep track of how many E2As you completed.

The great thing about the Poise Deck is that

you personally selected each E2A because it is something that would advance you toward your vision. That means you can reject or choose as many cards as you want and your choice will always be a productive one for you.

The Rules of the Game

Now that you know about The Poise Game, you should know that your game has begun.

The question is, "Will you play it well or not?"

To play The Poise Game well requires you to make deliberate and productive choices that lead you to become your ideal self and live your ideal life.

Here are the rules of the game:

1. Think about your vision. Your vision is the most ideal situation for you, so you should regularly contemplate it so that you experience it in your mental domain until you can experience it in the physical one.

2. Make a choice. Your choices are your choices. Recognize that no other person, being, or inanimate object makes you do anything.

Your choices include your thoughts, emotions, words and deeds. In a cyclical fashion, your thoughts produce emotions and emotions produce feelings and feelings produce words and words produce deeds that are consistent with the vision.

3. Express gratitude for the outcomes. If your choices belong to you, then your experiences do, too. They are often presented as outcomes relating to your choices.

Like a mathematical equation that produces results on the other side of the equal sign, in The Poise Game you acknowledge your inputs and assume that, if the results are perceptually desirable, then that is the result of the collective inputs. If the results are perceptually undesirable, then that is also the result of the collective inputs.

You must be grateful for that feedback and acknowledge that the only inputs you can control or modify are your own.

4. Share the game with others. People are social creatures. There's scientific evidence to support that our neural development is a function of the extent to which we experience social nurturing at pivotal points in our formative years. This demand for engagement doesn't cease. Therefore, you will recognize that it is impossible to achieve your vision without the assistance of others—direct or indirect.

The mandate to share the game with others allows you to introduce the concept of deliberately choosing to make yourself better, which means the collective society is better. If one more person that you share the game with decides to play, then you've improved more than just your life. You've contributed to the betterment of another. If the pattern of sharing and playing the game continues to spread, then we can only be excited about the society of people being their best selves and living their best lives.

Follow these four rules and you are a winner at The Poise Game.

Max Game-Mode

I want to reiterate that once you opened the pages of this book and realized the premise of The Poise Game is about choice, that was the moment you began playing the game.

You are playing The Poise Game right now.

I recommend you implement the game's tools and methods piecemeal as often as you can.

But there are a few distinct occasions when you'll likely want to go Max Game-Mode. Max Game-Mode is when you decide to play the game as prescribed starting at stage one.

Go Max Game-Mode when you encounter one of these five situations:

1. Free time. Free time is great to have, especially in a fast-paced world. However, free time can become counter-productive time if you find yourself idle or procrastinating.

The famed psychiatrist Dr. Carl Jung once said, "Were it not for the leaping and twinkling of the soul, man would rot away in his greatest passion, idleness."

You can combat the atrophy of your vision with deliberate use of The Poise Game tools and methods. You'll discover that your choices can include everything from exercise and meditation to work and rest. The key is that you play to make your choice.

2. Depression. It was during the time when I found myself in a state of despair that I was motivated to create this game, so it is certainly suitable for you if you find yourself experiencing depression.

Because the tools are tailored to that which is important to you and the methods are universally proven to generate gratitude, playing the game is a surefire way to combat and, eventually, overcome depression.

3. Discontent. Feeling discontentment about your situation is something most people experience at different seasons in their lives. However, if you discover this feeling is weighing you down and incapacitating productive thoughts, emotions, words and deeds, then playing the game will act as your medicine.

Making the choice to shuffle the Poise Deck and complete the selected E2As will give you small wins that can produce contentment.

4. Apathy. Many people incorrectly believe hate is the opposite emotion of love; but the true opposite of love is fear.

Love and hate are similar in that they are indicated by passion.

Fear is different. And one of the major indicators of fear is apathy, or carelessness.

If you begin to discover you're struggling to find joy or even displeasure in anything, then you are a strong candidate for playing The Poise Game with all of its bells and whistles. In this state, you will be searching for the smallest glimpse of light, the lightest touch, the faintest heartbeat, the slightest sign of life.

It's in you—somewhere.

Implement the graduated poise pattern starting at Vision Board and work your way through the stages engaging with your TAN until your wins begin to take root.

Through the roots, you will receive the sustenance you need to activate your senses, thereby re-energizing your passion for life.

5. Hopeful. If you're feeling positive and optimistic about your prospects, then you are primed to reinforce those sentiments by playing The Poise Game.

Playing the game and experiencing small wins as you choose to complete E2As and accomplish T2D Lists that lead to the achievement of your GAInS Adventures will give you tangible and real examples you can use to encourage you through difficult times that challenge your hope and energize you through trouble-free times when your hope is at its highest point.

Becoming a Winner in The Poise Game

21st century gaming has taken the world by storm. Using simple psychological and marketing techniques, people have become slaves to their digital devices—oftentimes neglecting to live their real lives in lieu of their faux life in the digital world.

The Poise Game makes living real-life addicting. You are your character.

You get to choose your quests. You can monitor your progress in relation to your vision. You can change your path and choose new goals, new aspirations and new initiatives to accomplish. Your imagination is permitted to translate into the physical domain.

You beat the game whenever you achieve your vision, and when you do that, your name is inscribed on the "Wall of Champions"—figuratively speaking, of course.

But, in reality, when you become your ideal self and live your ideal life, your vision will transform and your purpose will expand for you to experience another dimension of fulfillment.

Have you ever asked yourself how close you are to winning in the game of life?

You probably thought the illusive answer would indefinitely remain beyond your reach.

But now you can answer that question. And of all things that can help you do that, it's by playing a game.

The Poise Game subscribes to the belief that the most critical attribute for you to be able to achieve your desires is behavior modification via the deliberate development and practice of poise.

The game is designed to help you develop and demonstrate this critical attribute in a live game environment that can be played as often or as little as you need. Ultimately, using The Poise Game methods and tools will help you create productive instinctive habits that transform your experience from dependence upon playing your game to intuitively living your game. And your game inevitably leads to your ideal self and your ideal life.

You play The Poise Game to achieve your vision. Once that occurs, you can continue to play the game with a focus on sustainment, or your vision can evolve and then the game continues, this time with you aiming for a different vision for yourself and your life.

The exciting part about The Poise Game is that each time you play it, you get the experience of winning. Although the vision is the destination, and the goals, aspirations, and initiatives are the adventures, it's the exercise of your choice that makes you a winner.

Remember, you're playing this game because you are discontented with some aspect of your life and you want to believe it is possible to experience joy. Your joy comes through your awareness, acknowledgment, and acceptance of the responsibility that belongs to you and you alone—you choose who you are and the life you experience.

Demonstrating poise is how you win the game and win at life.

Your Character

"No man can begin to mould himself on a faith or an idea without rising to a higher order of experience."

George Eliot

Your first step to playing The Poise Game is to imagine and create your character.

Your character is your ideal self, which is the fully-realized version of you personifying the exact vision of yourself that where you are, you can do and you can possess everything you need.

This is one of the most important choices you must make when playing The Poise Game.

Remember, in chapter one you learned that the ideal self is the version of you that checks all your blocks regarding your aesthetics, attitudes, activities, affiliations and accomplishments. It's the manifestation of you that epitomizes everything you aspire to be. In this state there is perfect contentment and equilibrium.

You are afforded the freedom to design your character, choosing things like your personality, religion, appearance, interests, education level, occupation, relationships and socio-economic status.

Ultimately, when you review the attributes of your character, it should represent your grandest ideals about yourself.

It's worth noting that for the remainder of the book, I will use the terms character, best self, and ideal self interchangeably. Understand that in the context of gameplay, you are dealing with your character. However, in the broader context of The Poise Game, your character is authentically you—your best and most ideal self.

Now that we're on the same page with this, let's continue.

There's several ways you can present your character, but one of the things that I've learned is that when I feel like I have an infinite amount of options, I become incapacitated by decision paralysis.

To mitigate this, I recommend that when you play The Poise Game, you depict your character using something you may have heard about before.

That's right.

You're going to make a vision board.

Character Translation Techniques

If you're not an arts and crafts type of person, then I'm about to break your heart because you will need to manufacture your vision piece by piece to ensure you transfer the image of yourself that you envision inside your mind onto the physical poster board in some discerning way.

If you recall in chapter three, a few of the resources you collected included a poster board, a marker, scissors, tape, glue, and old newspapers and magazines. This is where those items will be used.

I must add this point. The objective here is to create a tangible representation of your ideal self, your Character, that you can see with your eyes.

If you have a guttural reaction to producing it via arts and crafts, but you feel capable of doing so using digital means, then feel free to create it that way. Just remember, what's in your head should be able to be viewed by another person. If that's not possible, then you've chosen to keep your vision of your character in a nebulous place that won't help when you're seeking external inspiration because you're unable to access the vision inside you.

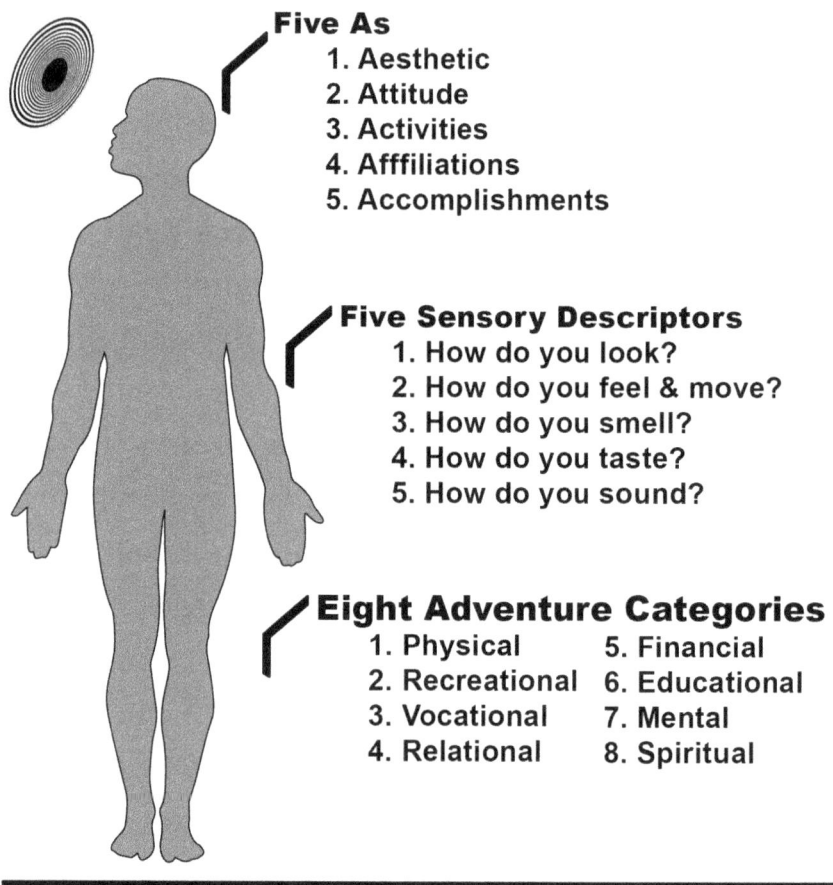

Character Translation Techniques

You can choose to keep your vision in your head, but I don't recommend it because there is power in seeing the visible display of who you choose to be. By doing so, you benefit from the experience of creating yourself. You benefit from ownership and pride with which you must exhibit to present yourself to others, especially those in your TAN. You benefit from being able to assess your current status, including your thoughts, emotions, words and deeds in comparison to how you would conduct yourself once you become your best version of you.

Being able to visually see your character allows you the freedom to draw those constructive critiques and the allowance to make adjustments to ensure it aligns with your desires.

I'm assuming you have a picture in mind of who you intend to become.

Now we need to transfer that image onto the physical plane so that you and anyone with whom you care to share it can see.

You will use three translation techniques to create your character in The Poise Game.

The first translation technique is the 'Five As.' This involves describing your character based upon five attributes: aesthetics, attitudes, activities, affiliations, and accomplishments.

The second translation technique is the 'Five Sensory Descriptors.' In short, this uses five questions based upon your five senses to solicit the descriptions of your ideal self.

The third translation technique is the 'Eight Adventure Attributes.' In short, this uses the eight adventure categories used for developing your GAInS to describe your best self.

The next three paragraphs describe the three translation techniques and guide you through using them. You can read to get an understanding of what they are, but I recommend you grab a pen and notebook to jot down observations that come to mind so you can use them later. It'll save you time, and also, there is often a certain level of purity in the first things that come to mind because you don't give yourself a chance to dilute or edit them based upon social contrivances.

Five A's

My experiences have taught me that there are five simple ways that you can describe yourself. As I discussed before, they are called the 'Five A's—the five attributes. By looking at your attributes, you can create a clear description of who you are.

The first attribute is aesthetics. Aesthetics are visual descriptions of yourself and answer questions such as: How do you generally look? Are you slim and trim, athletic or curvy? What is your style regarding apparel, footwear and accessories?

The second attribute is attitudes. Attitudes are perceptions that may be deduced from the manner in which you operate and answer questions such as: How do you carry yourself? How is your typical countenance? How do you respond to danger, excitement, romance, fun, grief and success?

The third attribute is activities. Activities are the things that you do and answer questions such as: What is your occupation? What do you do during free time? How do you learn and maintain information that interests you? What hobbies do you have? What duties do you perform based upon the roles.

The fourth attribute is affiliations. Affiliations are the people or organizations to whom you pledge your loyalties and answer questions such as: What person or group do you support? Of what groups are you a member or aspiring member? Which conferences or seminars do you attend and participate? To what causes do you donate money, time and other resources?

The fifth attribute is accomplishments. Accomplishments are the milestones that you achieve and answer questions such as: What degrees did you earn? What certifications or licensures do you have? What awards and recognitions were you nominated for and won? What are the things that received no external praise, but you're personally proud about?

The rule of thumb with these and the rest of the translation techniques is to allow yourself the freedom to envision what you believe is ideal and the freedom to choose your own attributes.

If nothing specific comes to mind with the prompts available, then exercise your freedom of choice to move to the next one or jump around, if you prefer. The Poise Game presents it this way so you can systematically cover each relevant point so you have the best opportunity to translate your character from your mind to physical medium.

Five Sensory Descriptors

It's amazing how much we're taught in our formative years to deny our senses. The sensory experiences that we have as children contribute to the most vivid experiences. Yet, there was often someone who would tell you that at some point you'll have to stop dreaming. At some point, you'd need to be realistic.

When using the 'Five Sensory Descriptors' technique, you'll need to tap into that youthful, uninhibited, undefiled energy to experience yourself as who you choose to become.

If it feels contrived or silly, keep going deeper into that mind-frame until you've gotten beyond the fabricated filters that sought to dampen your sensibilities.

Find the part of you that didn't care what other people thought or said because those things you sensed were real to you.

If you're struggling to get there just imagine for a moment what your experience would be if you were there, allow that to guide you as you search for the descriptors that will help you define your ideal self.

Now that you're there, find that three-dimensional mental image of your best self. We're going to use it to build your character.

As you observe it, answer these five questions:

How do you look?

Go ahead and walk around yourself. Look from afar and close-up. Look at your indifferent facial expression. Look at your smile. Look at your frown. Look at your furrowed brow. You can see something that's notable, remarkable, distinguishable, otherwise interesting about you in your best form. Take note of what you sense.

How do you feel and move?

Reach out and make contact with yourself. Take note of your constitution. Look at your posture. Look at your presence. Direct yourself to move. You can feel the quality and fluidity of your locomotion. You know intuitively what it means regarding your wellness, faculty, confidence and lifestyle. Take note of what you sense.

How do you smell?

Get closer again and take a deep breath. Don't be afraid to write something down even if it's faint. Take note of what you sense.

How do you taste?

I'm not recommending that you lick your mental image, but I do ask that you get as close as possible and focus on what you taste. Your descriptions might include sweet, sour, salty, acidic, savory, bitter or spicy. Take note of what you sense.

How do you sound?

Listen to yourself speak, hum or sing, whisper, shout, cry, laugh and breathe. Take a note of what you sense.

Let me repeat that the rule of thumb with these and the rest of the translation techniques is to not get stuck on any one.

While I recommend you explore all aspects to create the fullest representation of your character, I

> Sam's Character: Vision Board Part I
>
> Five A's
> A1 Cool nerdy; 90's retro; Slim; broad shoulders
> A2 Dry humor; quiet; serious; mysterious
> A3 Musician; bio-engineer
> A4 Church; boy scouts; National Society of Professional Engineers;
> UCSD A5 Professional Engineer; Fundamentals of Engineering
>
> Five Sensory Descriptors
> Look - happy and confident
> Feel/move - firm; smooth; methodological gait
> Smell - apple cinnamon; autumn
> Taste - sour; salty; spicy
> Sound - airy and harmonious
>
> Eight Adventure Categories
> 1 Physical - golfer
> 2 Recreation - musician; pianist
> 3 Vocational - bio-engineer
> 4 Relational - married w/ 1 child; vacations in U.S. Virgin Islands
> 5 Financial - upper middle class
> 6 Educational - Ph. D. Bio-Engineering; Full Scholarship
> 7 Mental - skeptic
> 8 Spiritual - music ministry; missionary work in Africa

Character Translation Techniques Examples

also know that working with the little bit you have is better than not working with anything at all. In this case, something is better than nothing.

Eight Adventure Attributes

The 'Eight Adventure Attributes' are very important to The Poise Game because they form the framework of the GAInS. That's also why using them to create your character is prudent.

If you gave an effort with the previous two translation techniques, then you may have several key elements that represent your ideal self that you can use on your Vision Board, probably with minor adjustments. Using the 'Eight Adventure Attributes' should help you to finalize your character with attributes that you can systematically attain.

The attributes are:

1. Physical. Physical attributes comprise items such as aesthetics, functionality and health. In other words, they represent how you look, what you can do and how healthy you are.

2. Recreational. Recreational attributes comprise items such as your hobbies, extracurricular activities, social affiliations and any interests not specifically addressed in the other categories.

3. Vocational. Vocational attributes comprise items such as your career, any additional occupations, entrepreneurial interests, business ownership and leadership positions.

4. Relational. Relational attributes comprise items such as relationship status, parental status and preferences for social interactions.

5. Financial. Financial attributes comprise items

such as income, investments, retirement plan, credit worthiness, debt, royalties and intellectual property.

6. Educational. Educational attributes comprise items such as degrees, schools attended, certifications, licenses, accreditations and other credentials.

7. Mental. Mental attributes comprise items such as philosophical practices and beliefs and worldview regarding human rights, economy, environment, politics, education, entertainment, justice and religion.

8. Spiritual. Spiritual attributes comprise items such as faith practices and beliefs and worldview regarding human rights, economy, environment, politics, education, entertainment, justice and religion.

In some ways the mental and spiritual attributes can overlap.

If you are a person who doesn't subscribe to spirituality, then you can forego the spiritual attributes. If you are a spiritually-inclined person who subscribes to the opinion that your mental attributes and spiritual attributes are the same, then you can forego the mental attributes.

Although the mental and spiritual attributes are similar, they are certainly mutually exclusive. I am a spiritual person and I can find attributes that fall into the mental category.

For example, I describe my ideal self as a 'well-read man.' This is an attribute that, for me, is clearly a mental attribute, but doesn't fit exclusively into the spiritual category.

If you are a spiritual person who believes being well-read or other attributes of mental variety are a function of your spirituality, then perhaps, you would assign that attribute to the spiritual category and discover that the mental category is one you do not need.

I've attempted to make the categories as distinct as possible, but also as flexible as possible so that you can easily tailor them to your personal needs.

As stated above, the rule of thumb with the translation techniques is to not get stuck on them.

I recommend that you go through each translation technique a few times. This will help you to refine your character's attributes. In some cases you may realize that your ideal self has too much happening.

Personally, I'm an ambitious person so I can't judge, but you can. If it seems like too much, but it's all things you desire, then my recommendation is that you keep them. If it's too much and skirting the edge of your desires, you can nix them. It's your choice.

It's important to note that you're creating a future version of your ideal self in terms of timeframes, this could be you in no sooner than two years, but it could also be you 50 years from now if you prefer.

I'd recommend you create your character to be about three to five years from current if you want to envision yourself in the near term. I recommend you create your character to be about five to 10 years from current if you want to envision yourself in the midterm. I recommend you create your character to be about 10 to 20 years from current if you want to envision yourself in the long term.

This chapter focused on starting your Vision Board by creating your character, your ideal self. In the next chapter you will complete your Vision Board by creating your world, your ideal life.

This is the environment and external situations in which your character thrives.

Now that you know how to make your character, let's go make your world.

Your World

"The world you desire can be won, it exists, it is real, it is possible, it is yours."

Ayn Rand

Your next step to playing The Poise Game is to imagine and create your world.

Your world is your ideal life, the environment where all conditions are perfectly suited to your desires.

This bit that we're working on to create your Vision Board is important because it creates the terrain in which your character operates.

In chapter one you learned that the ideal life is the version of your life that checks all your blocks regarding relationships, resources, recreations and regions. You lack nothing your heart desires because you know that it is already within your possession or it will arrive at the exact moment when you need it.

The work you'll do in this chapter is a continuation of what you've already done except this time we'll focus on the ideal life. Similar to the way you extracted the elements from your mind in chapter four, we'll need to transfer those images into the physical plane again.

World Translation Techniques

You will use two translation techniques to create your world.

One of them is completely different, while the other one is similar to what you used in chapter four. The slight difference in these prompts is because instead of focusing on creating your character you're focusing on your world.

The first translation technique is the 'Environmental Factors.' These include characteristics relating to the physical space you intend to occupy in your ideal state. The 'Environmental Factors' are atmosphere, domicile, topography, neighborhood, residence and climate.

The second is the 'Five Sensory Descriptors,' with which you're already familiar.

The next two sections describe the two translation techniques used to create your world.

Similar to chapter four, I recommend you get a

Your World

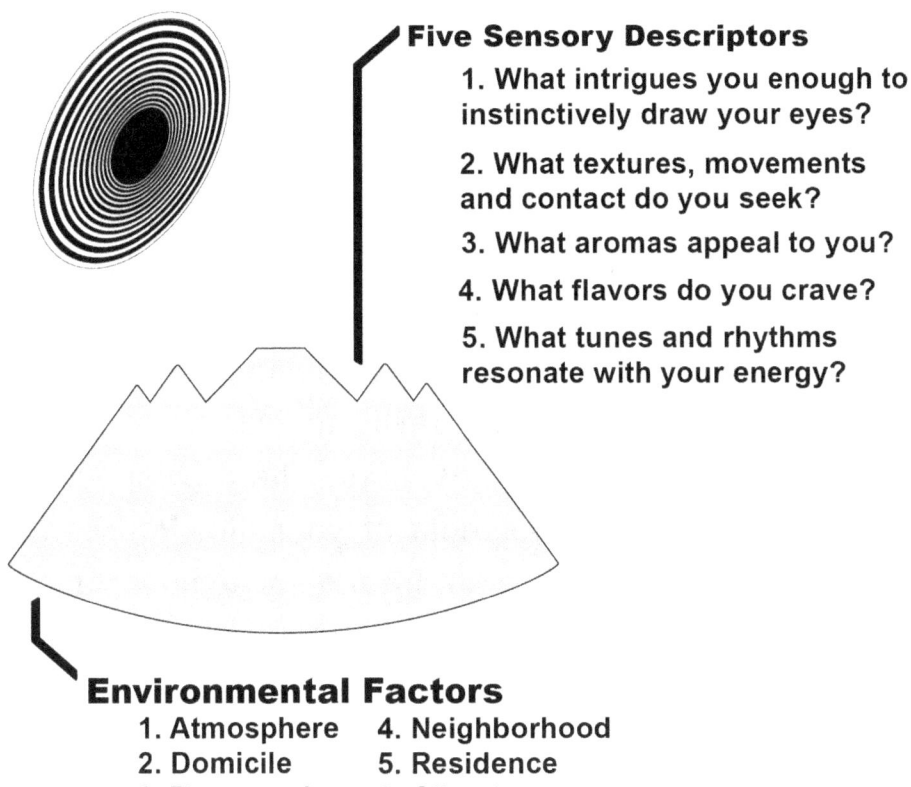

Five Sensory Descriptors
1. What intrigues you enough to instinctively draw your eyes?
2. What textures, movements and contact do you seek?
3. What aromas appeal to you?
4. What flavors do you crave?
5. What tunes and rhythms resonate with your energy?

Environmental Factors
1. Atmosphere 4. Neighborhood
2. Domicile 5. Residence
3. Topography 6. Climate

Poise Aspirant looking into the Apogee

pen and notebook to list your observations so when you're ready to build your vision board, you have the requisite information you need.

Environmental Factors

When considering the best possible terrain where your character will live, work and play, there are a few details about the terrain that you should seek to identify. I call them 'The 'Environmental Factors.' As you migrate through the list, use the 'Environmental Factors' to visualize the best, worst and unremarkable days in your world. Sense how you feel in that moment and then make a note of it.

By looking at these factors, including atmosphere, domicile, topography, neighborhood, residence and climate, you can create a clear description of the environment in which you desire to live.

The first factor is atmosphere. The atmosphere describes the auric aspects of your life. You can depict it as an energy field, frequency, temperature or color. It can be characterized based upon how permeable it is, its density and its conductivity.

The second factor is domicile. The domicile describes the locations in terms of nation-state. In which sovereign nations do you intend to reside. This will shape the languages, cultures and customs into which you immerse yourself.

The third factor is topography. The topography describes the physical landscape. How would you describe the terrain?

The fourth factor is neighborhood. The neighborhood describes the type of community in which you reside. The three general types of neighborhoods are urban, suburban and rural.

The fifth factor is residence. The residence describes the type of structure in which you choose to dwell. Simply put: where do you eat, store your belongings and sleep? This could be a house, cave, apartment, condo, shanty, RV or anything that fits into your vision of the ideal life.

The sixth factor is climate. The climate describes the seasons and weather of your world.

One of the key things about the 'Environmental Factors' is that you can verify them with reality checks. For example, if you're imagining living in Siberia, a domicile factor, and also envisioning tropical weather, a climate factor, then you must make an adjustment to one or the other because they are incongruent, which means your world—your ideal life—doesn't match reality.

As I suggested earlier, it's prudent for you to use the 'Environmental Factors' to visualize your best day, worst and your average day when you are living your ideal life. Free your mind to experience the stimulation of all of your senses, then record it.

It's worth noting that when you determine what your world comprises based upon the 'Environmental Factors,' you will need to also determine how you

> **Sam's World: Vision Board Part 2**
>
> <u>Environmental Factors</u>
> 1. Atmosphere - electric; light; free flowing
> 2. Domicile - USA
> 3. Topography - Flat; sea level elevation
> 4. Neighborhood - Urban
> 5. Residence - Condo
> 6. Climate - humid: hot; non-snowy winters
>
> <u>Five Sensory Descriptors</u>
> Intrigues the eyes - vibrant earth-tone and natural colors
> Textures and movements - warm sea breeze; fluid and effortless
> Aromas - coffee beans and lavender
> Palette - sweet and sour; acidic
> Tunes - Classical music; grand piano and strings
>
> <u>Personal Mission Statement (PMS)</u>
> I am a purveyor of knowledge and follow the facts wherever they lead me. I fear no set-backs, detours, dead-ends or failures because each one brings me closer to the truth I seek. I work, play and love hard because I intentionally live life to the fullest.
>
> <u>Personal Conviction Mantra (PCM)</u>
> I know the truth and it sets me free

World Translation Techniques Examples

want to depict those elements on your Vision Board.

You're free to use words, but your mind prefers pictures. I recommend you find an image that can represent each element to ensure your world is completely realized in the Vision Board.

The more complete it is, the better the tool will be for times of reflection, times of motivation and times of accountability.

Five Sensory Descriptors

I mentioned above that some of the translation techniques for designing your world would be similar to those used to create your character. Now you'll use the 'Five Sensory Descriptors,' which in chapter four helped you to describe your ideal self. The difference here is that there are some modifications to the questions that shift the focus to describing the world and the environment in which you intend to live.

I invite you to once again go ahead and tap into that youthful, uninhibited and undefiled energy so this time you can experience your life as you choose it to be.

Now that you're there, find that three-dimensional mental image of your best life. We're going to use it to build your world.

As you observe it, answer these five questions:

What intrigues you enough to instinctively draw your eyes?

Something catches your eyes. It's the colors, patterns, brightness and sizes. Take note of what you sense.

What textures, movements and contact do you seek?

You can feel the temperature. You can feel the motions and currents. You can feel the mass and intensity that impacts you. Take note of what you sense.

What aromas appeal to you?

The scents beckon you. They arouse your emotions, appetite and libido. Take note of what you sense.

What flavors do you crave?

Perhaps you crave something sweet or sour or salty or acidic or savory or bitter or spicy. You cherish each morsel as it satisfies your palette. Take note of what you sense.

What tunes and rhythms resonate with your energy?

There is a soundtrack playing that compliments each moment you experience. Take note of what you sense.

Let me repeat that the rule of thumb from chapter four, don't get stuck on these. If nothing comes to you that fits, then move on to the next item.

You are not bound by these. They're simply prompts to generate mental imagery that you can transfer from your mind onto a physical representation using a Vision Board or digital display, if you're technologically inclined.

The main thing is to get it out of your head so you can review it and share it with someone, if you'd like.

And the neat thing is that, since it's yours, you can make it however you'd like it to be.

Find Pictures to Match the Words

If you navigated through these translation techniques, then you're able to begin selecting pictures to match your descriptions so you can complete your Vision Board so that it fully represents your ideal self and ideal life.

Vision Board

There are many ways you can accomplish this, but I'll describe a couple to give you some ideas to work with to get you started on your way.

Take your answers to the above prompts and conduct a search for the best images and pictures to represent those items and concepts. You are going to make a photo collage of all of these elements.

It's okay if you're a literal person to use pictures that depict exactly what you envisioned. For instance, if you envisioned your ideal self earning a doctorate degree, then you could choose to use a photo of a person receiving a doctorate degree at graduation or you could simply use a photograph of a doctoral degree diploma.

It's also okay if you're a symbolic person and choose to use pictures that symbolically represent what you envision. For example, if you envisioned an aspect of your ideal life including you living in Argentina and Brazil, then you could incorporate an image of a gaucho, which is the Spanish word for cowboy, since Argentina is known for its cattle, and an image of Carnival, an annual Brazilian celebration.

If you're opting to make the physical Vision Board, then you can also search the Internet for the corresponding images and print them. Honestly, that's probably the most expeditious way to find your images.

If you decide to create the digital Vision Board, then you can find all your photos online, paste or import them into a document, and then arrange them as you prefer.

The only way to mess up the creation of your Vision Board is if you don't create it.

Your Mission and Mantra

Once you have the visual aspects in place, then there are a couple more items that accompany your Vision Board—the Personal Mission Statement and the Personal Conviction Mantra. These may appear to be extra, but they help you to communicate your narrative associated with the imagery and helps to guide your actions toward the desired outcomes.

The Personal Mission Statement or PMS is a short paragraph, between two to six sentences, that highlights your visionary mandate for yourself and your life. It is your statement that conveys the spirit of your efforts. It guides your thoughts, emotions, words and deeds to be productive incremental contributions to bringing your vision into fruition.

One of my favorite books is The Alchemist by Paulo Coelho. In his book, Coelho tells a story of a boy who sets out on a journey to discover his life's purpose, but by the end of his journey, the boy learned so much more than he'd imagined. He learned how everything was created by the same hand; therefore, all things are designed to work in harmony.

The idea that everything is codependent because everything is one fed into his life mission, which Coelho referred to as his personal legend. The PMS drives you to reinforce the certainty of your vision so that the gap between the present and the ideal situations steadily closes.

The final piece to your Vision Board puzzle is the Personal Conviction Mantra or PCM. The Personal Conviction Mantra is a short saying that you can use as a deliberate trigger to focus your thoughts, emotions, words and deeds on your vision. It can be one word, a few words, or an entire sentence.

Think of it as a slogan or tagline.

It should be something you can easily memorize and something that resonates with you when thought or spoken. Its purpose is to disrupt any efforts that are counterproductive or inconsistent with your vision.

If you have a notepad and something with which to write, a smartphone, a tablet, a computer, or something to record you speaking nearby, why don't you take a moment to draft your PMS and PCM.

It's okay if you feel it's rough and needs some revision. Treat the effort of starting as an E2A and log it as a win for yourself.

By the way, you shouldn't feel any pressure or self-judgment. If you're struggling with one, the other, or both, then choose to give yourself some time to think about it.

You may be wondering if you can display your Vision Board without the PMS and PCM.

Yes, you can still display your Vision Board without these items; but, as with the other recommended tools, the strength and quality of your game play will be in direct proportion to the completeness and quality of your tools. And don't forget that in this game, when you win, it means you win in real life.

If you completed this chapter and recorded your observations in response to the prompts, then you have the information to create your Vision Board. If you took your notes and identified images to represent them and developed your PMS and PCM, then your Vision Board Display is complete.

Take the time to review it to ensure it presents your ideal self and ideal life. It's possible that you unintentionally included things that reflect another person's projections upon you and those elements aren't something you'd like to pick for yourself. If that's the case, you have the freedom and option to erase anything that isn't your desire.

And your visual depiction can be literal, metaphorical, or a combination of the two.

Invest your effort into making your Vision Board. It doesn't need to be perfect. It just needs to be started.

Once you make the initial transfer of thoughts from your head to an external medium, then I'm certain you'll follow through and produce a vision board that has utility for you. And you can update, modify, overhaul, or whatever you believe is the appropriate approach to using it and refining it through the years.

You can find more details regarding how to create a Vision Board display with PMS and PCM in the section called 'The Poise Game Tools.'

Free templates can be downloaded at www.poisegame.com.

In this chapter, you learned how to create the Vision Board. In the next chapter, you will build and learn how to use several more of your Poise Game tools.

Your Tools

"Success depends upon previous preparation, and without such preparation there is sure to be failure."

Confucius

Can you play The Poise Game without taking the time to make your Vision Board?

Perhaps.

However, I strongly recommend against it because having a visual depiction of what you're shooting for is important to keep you on the chosen path.

Plus, you cannot get around creating the tools listed in this chapter if you intend to play The Poise Game.

So, if you don't care about the theory behind playing The Poise Game and just want to get straight to playing and making progress toward your desired outcomes, then this chapter is where you want to be.

Disclaimer—this chapter will require you to do some work to build the requisite tools you'll need to begin playing.

They are the bread and butter for helping you discover, make progress toward, and attain your desired outcomes.

But once the tools are created, then, unless you fundamentally change your mind, they should be good for at least the next year, and possibly more.

What's also special about these tools is that they are designed to complement the methods you will learn later. The methods presented in later chapters can be used by themselves, but their effectiveness is enhanced when employing them with the tools in this chapter.

Bottom-line: Make your tools so you can get to playing the game and playing it most effectively.

Making Your GAInS

The Goals, Aspirations, and Initiatives Structure or GAInS, organizes predetermined annual adventures into one of eight adventure categories:

1. Physical. Physical adventures include objectives relating to your body's aesthetics, functionality and health.

2. Recreational. Recreational adventures include

objectives relating to your hobbies, extracurricular activities, social affiliations, and any interests not specifically addressed in the other categories.

3. Vocational. Vocational adventures include objectives relating to your career, secondary occupations, entrepreneurial interests, business ownership, and leadership positions.

4. Relational. Relational adventures include objectives relating to relationship status, parental status, and preferences for social interactions.

5. Financial. Financial adventures include objectives relating to income, investments, retirement plans, credit worthiness, debt, royalties, and intellectual property.

6. Educational. Educational adventures include objectives relating to degrees, schools attended, certifications, licenses, accreditations and other credentials.

7. Mental. Mental adventures include objectives relating to philosophical practices and beliefs, and world views regarding human rights, economy, environment, politics, education, entertainment, justice and religion.

8. Spiritual. Spiritual adventures include

objectives relating to faith practices and beliefs, and world view regarding human rights, economy, environment, politics, education, entertainment, justice and religion.

GAInS Adventure List

SMART = SPECIFIC | MEASURABLE | ACHIEVABLE | RELEVANT | TIME-BOUND

- Join gym that has extended business hours, personal trainer and group training packages by 1 Feb.
- Reduce pant size from 36in to 34in waist by 1 Dec.
- Begin weekly lessons with a golf professional trainer by 1 June
- Try a new hairstyle that I haven't tried before by 21 Mar.
- Write and produce two original songs including instrumental and vocal arrangements by 1 Sep.
- Learn to play the bass guitar part for 3 songs without mistakes by 31 Dec.
- Complete the NCEES FE Other Disciplines Study Guide by 1 Oct.
- Pass the FE exam by 31 Dec.
- Take trip to U.S. Virgin Islands with at least one friend by 31 Dec.
- Increase credit score by 100 points using strategies that include reducing consumer CC debt by 31 Dec.
- Save a minimum of $15K in savings and/or brokerage account funds by 31 Dec.
- Submit application UC San Diego bio-engineering Ph. D. program by 1 Feb.
- Read 4 books about Greek Skepticism by 31 Dec.
- Invite a total of six people to attend Bible study with church fellowship by 31 Dec.
- Write and share a weekly devotional with others beginning by 1 Sep.

GAInS Adventure List Example

You will recognize these categories are familiar because they were used to develop your character portion of your Vision Board. The difference here is that instead of them being referred to as attributes, on the GAInS they are referred to as adventures.

In chapter four, you observed that mental and spiritual attributes can overlap. This also applies to mental and spiritual adventures. My opinion is that mental and spiritual adventures are mutually exclusive, but I acknowledge that you may believe the contrary.

Therefore, if you are not spiritual, then it's your prerogative to not choose any spiritual adventures. Also, if you're spiritual and believe that your mental and spiritual adventures are the same, then you can forego the mental adventures.

GAInS Adventures are created using a modified version of the SMART goal-setting method, which I call the SMART adventure-setting method.

The SMART adventure-setting method states that an adventure must be specific, measurable, achievable, relevant, and time-based. The modification that applies for The Poise Game is that each adventure must start with a verb or the specific action that you intend to perform followed by the remaining elements of the SMART adventure-setting method.

An example of a physical adventure would be 'Lose 15 pounds in six months through diet and exercise.' Let's verify that the adventure meets the specifications of the SMART adventure.

Is the adventure specific? Yes. By using the verb phrase, 'lose weight,' it depicts what I intend to do. By including the prepositional phrase, 'through diet and exercise,' it depicts the exact ways in which I intend to do it.

Is the adventure measurable? Yes. I intend to lose 15 pounds. By using a numerical value with a unit of measure, I can assess progress in comparison to my original start point. This means I will know whether or not the objective is reached.

Is the adventure achievable? Yes. I intend to lose 15 pounds in six months. Considering conventional standards of losing weight and assuming I am able to exercise and eat an appropriate diet, I'm able to determine that this adventure is achievable.

Is the adventure relevant? Yes. I intend to lose 15 pounds in six months. By reviewing my Vision Board or conferring with my personal mission statement, I can determine the relevance of this adventure.

Is the adventure time-based? Yes. I intend to lose 15 pounds in six months. By using a timeframe, the adventure has a definable suspense.

If it wasn't clear to you before, the GAInS is a

yearly product. The idea is that you establish it prior to the beginning of a new year so you're able to optimize every moment of the next year toward the accomplishment of the GAInS.

I recommend you identify at least one GAInS Adventure per category, but you can choose one adventure for the entire year, if that's your preference.

If you're an ambitious person but you also respond negatively when you're unable to complete a list of objectives, then please consider practicing some restraint.

While I'm sure you're more than capable of accomplishing an ambitious list, take some time to consider the feasibility of your endeavor.

It's up to you, but this is a drill designed to set you up for winning.

And winning is no fun, if it's no fun.

Now don't be discouraged by my recommendations above.

If you're feeling motivated, then make a robust GAInS because there is no penalty if you select several adventures per category and don't successfully complete them during the year.

There may be a self-imposed psychological

penalty for which you'll need to muster some perseverance to manage, but that shouldn't negatively impact your drive or ambition.

There is no need to be afraid of being ambitious about becoming your best self and living your best life.

The GAInS helps you to make a choice regarding what's important and to be accountable and aware of areas that may lack balance because you've chosen to emphasize some and disregard others. It is the roadmap that leads you to your desired outcomes.

T2D List

The Things to Do (T2D) List is a useful tool for The Poise Game Aspirants who want to organize their daily, monthly, or quarterly activities. This is basically a task list of items that you intend to accomplish.

The difference between your T2D List and your standard task list is that the former contains Efficient and Effective Activities (E2As), which are tasks directly linked to the accomplishment of one of your GAInS Adventures or support the attainment of your ideal self and ideal life as portrayed by your Vision Board.

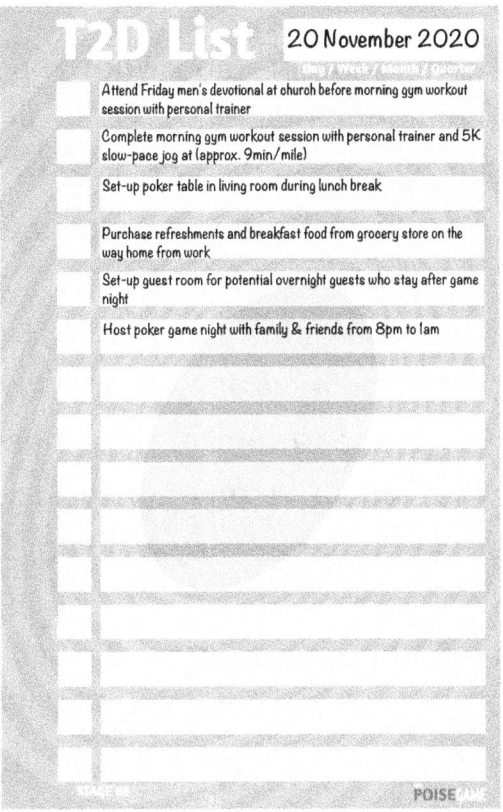

T2D List Example

To make your T2D List, you simply need to consider which GAInS Adventures or Vision Board images you'd like to work toward, then select E2As to perform that relate to the selected objectives.

This can be produced simply on a notepad or it can be digitally produced using a word processor or a software application.

There are a few keys to success for using the

T2D List.

First, you must understand what you're working toward. I recommend using the GAInS to guide you, but either way, you should be deliberate about what you are aiming for with the selected E2As on this list.

Second, pre-determine the time frame in which you're working. I believe daily or weekly T2D Lists are easiest to manage and are the best pacer for assessing whether you're on track to accomplish the task in a timely manner as they relate to subsequent E2As for specific adventures.

Third, keep the list short and succinct. While your GAInS can be ambitious, the T2D List must reflect your restraint because it's important that you direct your energies appropriately to each task to see them through to completion.

Later in chapter 10, you'll learn more about this concept when I introduce you to The Poise Game method that encourages you to prioritize rather than compromise.

Write your T2D Lists anywhere and everywhere that makes sense for you. Write them on pocket calendars, notebooks, home or office dry erase boards, or a mobile application.

You want the T2D List to be written somewhere that fits into your daily schedule and that you will naturally encounter so it serves its most important functions, which are to focus your attention, drive your actions, and hold you accountable to your vision.

You are interested in The Poise Game because you are searching for a nudge, a boost of energy, purpose and direction that leads you toward becoming your best self and living your best life.

E2As

The Efficient and Effective Activities (E2As) represent the basic building blocks of the ideal self and ideal life. They are the deliberate actions that lead to productivity and progress based upon your personal definition of success.

If you understand how to create GAInS Adventures, then creating E2As will be simple for you at this point because the format is the same.

Just apply the SMART adventure-setting method to ensure each E2A is specific, measurable, achievable, relevant, and time-based, and you're 99 percent done.

The major difference between a GAInS Adventure and an E2A is that the E2A is a thought or action that contributes to the completion of a GAInS Adventure.

There are two types of E2As—custom and generic.

The custom E2As follow the SMART format and are used in conjunction with the Vision Board, the GAInS, or on the T2D List. These can be generated in advance or created at the time that you're playing the relevant stages of the game.

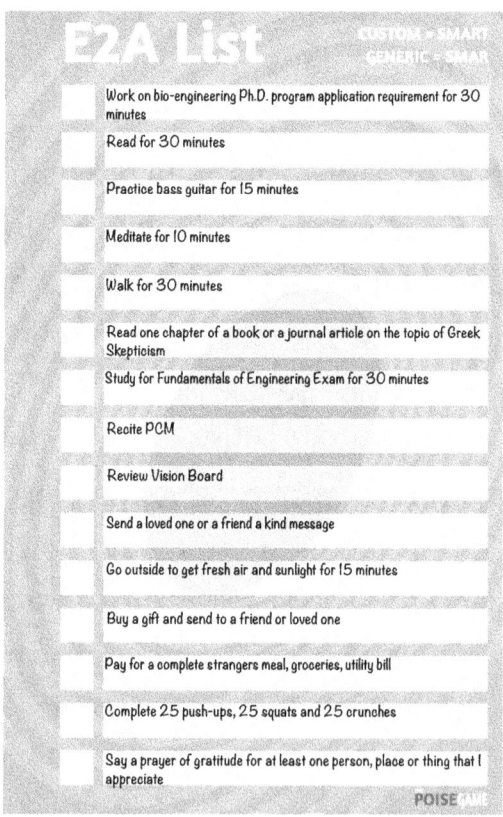

E2A) List Example

The generic E2As are pre-written thoughts and actions that lead to the accomplishment of a GAInS Adventure or the attainment of your ideal self and life. These may be used in conjunction with the Vision Board or on the T2D List, but they are mostly used as the items that form the Poise Deck.

Let's look at an example that shows the difference between a custom and generic E2A.

In this example, both E2As are designed to contribute toward the achievement of an educational GAInS Adventure.

An example custom E2A would be "Call the University of Texas Clinical Psychology doctoral program graduate admissions office to obtain answers to your questions about teaching assistantship opportunities no later than close of business hours this Friday." You can see that this custom E2A meets all the requirements. It's specific, measurable, achievable, relevant, and time-based. It's obviously custom because it addresses action details that are tailored for a certain outcome.

An example generic E2A would be "Study for the GRE for 60 minutes." You can see that this generic E2A meets all the requirements, except that it doesn't explicitly state the time-based component.

The reason is because the generic E2A time-component is dependent upon whichever tool is used. If used with the T2D List, then you can set the time suspense based upon the list's timeframe. If used in the Poise Deck, then your suspense is at the moment when you draw the card and choose to complete the action.

Remember, your list of E2As can be endless as long as they contribute to you becoming your best self and living your best life.

Keep a notebook or electronic document that has your running list of custom and generic E2As. You can use it to update your GAInS, plan T2D Lists in advance, or refresh your Poise Deck. And, as with everything in The Poise Game, if something doesn't match your desires or your preferences, then you have the freedom to change it.

The Poise Deck

The Poise Deck is the card-based implement of The Poise Game. The purpose of the Poise Deck is to reduce your set of choices to a finite amount of options that you know will be productive.

It rehearses your mental muscles that contribute deliberately to decision-making and demonstrations of self-control, using what amounts to a standard deck of cards.

Poise Deck Example

When making your Poise Deck, I recommend keeping it simple and sticking with a traditional 52-playing card deck. However, the Poise Deck consists of as many cards as you prefer.

On the face side of each card contains an E2A that you placed either by using sticky labels or some other means. If you're inclined, you can use a custom card-making software or website to produce your Poise Deck.

Remember that the deck comprises generic E2As that lead to the accomplishment of the annual GAInS Adventures. It's possible that some cards will have enduring generic E2As, but be prepared to produce additional cards or decks as you make progress toward becoming your ideal self and living your ideal life.

The simplest way to make your Poise Deck is to write a list of generic E2As. The list can be as long as you prefer as long as it corresponds with your Vision Board.

When you look at the individual images on your Vision Board, think about simple actions that you can do that would lead to that picture becoming a reality. Write those actions down using the generic E2A format described earlier.

Your list should also consist of generic E2As that support your GAInS Adventures. Start with the first category and work your way through all eight, writing down each activity you could do to accomplish the specific items listed in the GAInS Adventure categories.

Your list should also include generic E2As that prompt you to practice some of The Poise Game methods.

You will learn about the methods in later chapters, but they are designed to condition your mind-frame and set your perspective to make deliberate choices related to your desired outcomes.

After you've written the list of generic E2As, then you can select the ones you prefer to include in your deck. If you don't have enough to complete a 52-card deck, then, when you make your labels, you can make duplicates of the E2As that you wouldn't mind increasing your chances of selecting. If you have more E2As than can fit on a 52-card deck, you can either prioritize the ones you prefer to do when playing The Poise Game at stage four or you can create multiple Poise Decks to accommodate all of your generic E2As.

I recommend that you include at least one generic E2A per GAInS Adventure category.

I prefer to write my generic E2As on sticky labels, but there are ways you can type and print them onto sticky labels. Once your labels are made, you can attach them to the cards, and you're Poise Deck is ready for game-time.

Identifying Your Powers

In chapter four when you envisioned your character, you described your ideal self in several ways to tease out a complete picture.

One of the things you didn't do is explicitly highlight your notable skills, talents, qualities and abilities—your powers.

These are things that you will use and leverage along your journey. You will aim to maintain or develop them more thoroughly as you achieve your adventures.

Your powers can be anything from interpersonal abilities such as charisma to technology skills like computer programming. If you want to list your physical power as super strength because you're capable of lifting heavy things, then feel free.

The powers, when used appropriately and in the proper context, can be your greatest strengths. However, when misused or abused, they can be your worst weakness.

The way you determine if your power is a strength or a weakness is if it contributes toward, or inhibits your desired outcomes.

Think about your go-to moves.

Think about those things that you can do easily that seem to give others difficulties.

Think about the things you do that are the reason people come to you.

Think about those things you worked hard to develop.

Think about the things you can do well that give you the most pride.

Think about some of your unassuming qualities that may be passive, but help to generate internal fortitude.

You can write as many as you want, but I believe a reasonable range is one to five powers listed. Use a notebook or electronic document to record your powers.

Managing Your Triggers

You created a picture of your world in chapter five that represented your ideal life.

The entire premise of The Poise Game is that by developing and using self-control, you can choose to become your best self and live your best life.

When you're focusing on the desirable aspects of anything, what's typically left out is the undesirables.

In this case, we will not focus on weaknesses because I believe weakness is a perceptual judgment that can easily change if conditions, including your perspective, change. Instead, you will identify your triggers, which represent the sensitive areas and topics that can cause you to respond instinctively in an unproductive way.

The reason your triggers exist isn't really important. You can spend a lifetime investigating your various hot-button areas and only arrive at the conclusion that they are deeper and more ingrained than you thought.

For The Poise Game, you will contemplate things that instinctively upset you. They could be what you might refer to as pet-peeves or personal taboos.

You're looking for behaviors and situations that cause you discomfort to the point that they influence your subsequent actions without much contemplation. You're also looking for those items that initiate a process of impassioned thinking that builds energy until the intensity requires some type of action to release the tension.

Examples can include hearing a certain word or phrase. It could also be a specific type of situation. One of your triggers may relate to how someone engages you, such as shouting at you.

The reason you want to know and identify your triggers is because they can be the impetus for self-inflicted obstacles to your progress. For that reason, you are going to use self-control, poise, to mitigate their potential negative effects by developing secondary triggers.

It's fair to assume that your triggers were created instinctively with the intent to protect you. They were made to prioritize self-preservation at any cost. That's why you shouldn't try to get rid of your triggers; you should learn to assess them for relevance. The assessment can come by way of the secondary trigger. From this perspective, you are respecting your triggers and the reason they exist.

The secondary trigger releases upon the experience of one of these identified triggers, then it allows you to analyze whether the response to the trigger will be productive or counterproductive. If your assessment determines that the trigger response will be productive, meaning it contributes to your vision, then you follow through as intended.

If your assessment determines that the trigger response will be counterproductive, then you can choose a more appropriate thought, emotion, word, or deed.

In this way, your triggers aren't weaknesses, unless you choose to let them be. As an Aspirant, I'm sure you intend to develop the poise to choose to make them strengths.

Setting Up Your Poise Aspirant Dashboard

The Poise Aspirant Dashboard can be thought of as a control panel for you and your life. It is composed of your tools and additional information in a single place for quick reference to facilitate your gameplay. This will assist you when you want to reflect upon your vision, review it for relevance, or take account of your accomplished adventures and those yet to be achieved.

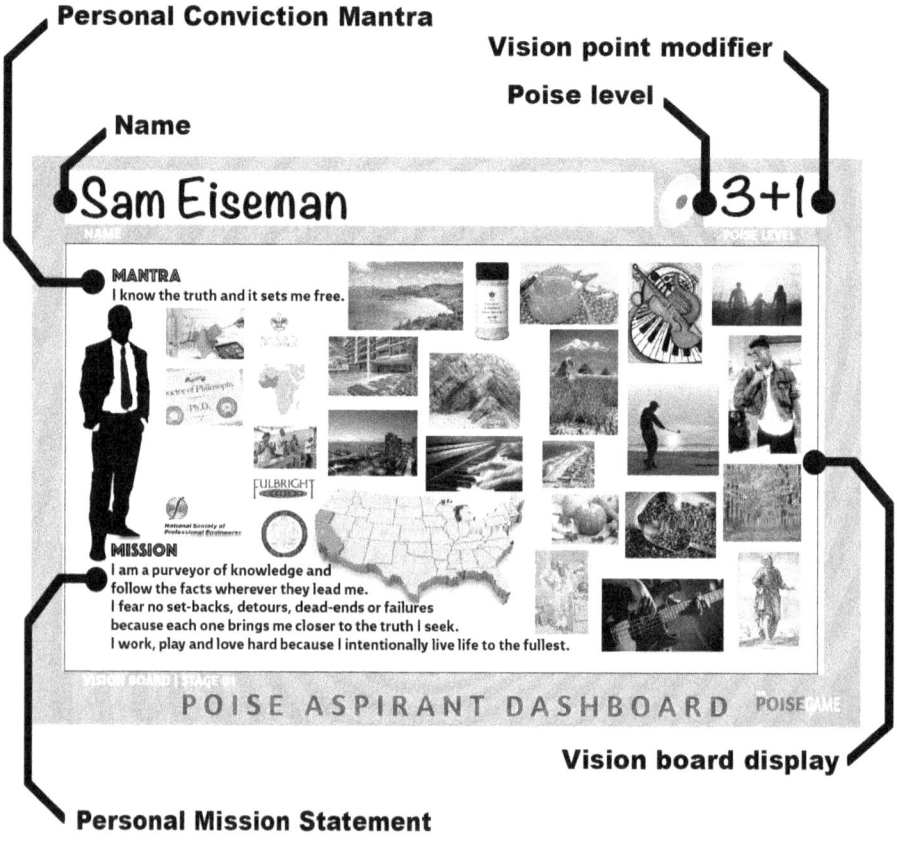

Vision Board | Front Side

The items that can be found on the Poise Aspirant Dashboard include:

Front Side

• *Name.* List what you prefer to be called. This is an important step because what you choose to be called is one of the most powerful creative decisions you make to energize progress toward attaining the ideal self and life you envision.

• ***Vision Board with Personal Mission Statement and Personal Conviction Mantra.*** The Vision Board image is either above or below your name and covers the remainder of the front side of the Poise Aspirant Dashboard.

• *Poise Level.* This is your current level in The Poise Game. Requirements regarding level ranking and how to advance to the next levels are found in chapter three.

Back Side

• *GAInS.* This is the current year's GAInS. Since the GAInS renews each year, you must update your Poise Aspirant Dashboard at least once every year. GAInS Adventures are written in an abbreviated format based upon space. The long format following the SMART Adventure-setting method is found in the GAInS Adventure Sheet. There is an empty block next to each GAInS Adventure. Upon completion, you can fill in the block and earn an adventure point.

• **Vision Points.** Each completed image on the Vision Board equals one vision point. These are important because they are a tally of your progress toward becoming your ideal self or living your ideal life. Each year when you update your Poise Aspirant Dashboard and GAInS, you update your current Poise level to reflect your vision points. To include vision points in your Poise Level, you add a plus sign (+) and then the current number of vision points accumulated. For example, a Poise level five Aspirant with three vision points is written as follows in the Poise level section: 5+3. This is updated once per year, so during the year if you achieve another Vision Board image and earn a vision point, then you will record it in the Vision Points section.

• **Adventure Points.** Each completed GAInS Adventure equals one adventure point. These are important because if you do not complete the annual GAInS, then your adventure points can carry over to the next year with the new

Poise Aspirant Dashboard. If you accumulate the requisite amount of adventure points, you can exchange them to level-up based upon the level-up guidelines.

• **E2A Points.** Each completed E2A equals one E2A point. This is where you keep track of your completed custom and generic E2As. Similar to the adventure points, these can carry over to the next year's Poise Aspirant Dashboard, which is required because each year your GAInS expires. If you accumulate the requisite amount of E2A points, you can exchange them to level-up based upon the level-up guidelines.

• **Victor Score.** This is a count of productive choices you've made despite difficult circumstances. You can add a point to your Victor score whenever you sense a desire to think, emote, speak, or act unproductively in relation to your vision, but instead, you make a choice that is productive.

• **Priorities.** In the event you have to make a choice between activities, this list of no more than 10 items provides guidance for your decisions based upon what's most important to you.

• **Powers.** This is the list of your identified powers

that you employ to complete E2As and make progress toward your vision. The card forces you to select your top-ranked powers to display. It's okay if you have several more powers that aren't depicted.

• **Triggers.** This is the list of your identified triggers for which you intend to deliberately exercise caution and restraint. These are not weaknesses, unless your response to them is counterproductive in relation to your vision. Once again, you may have several, but the limited space on the card forces you to select the ones you prefer to display. I recognize that you may be reluctant to display any of your triggers. You should know that I can empathize with your reservations. Only display what you are comfortable with displaying. If that means your triggers section is blank, then that's fine. You can still be mindful of them and leverage your TAN to mitigate their negative impact upon the attainment of your vision. You can also list triggers that are troublesome, but not ones you have concerns about displaying.

• **TAN.** This is the list of people who you trust and who have your best interests at heart. They are the people who play important roles in your life

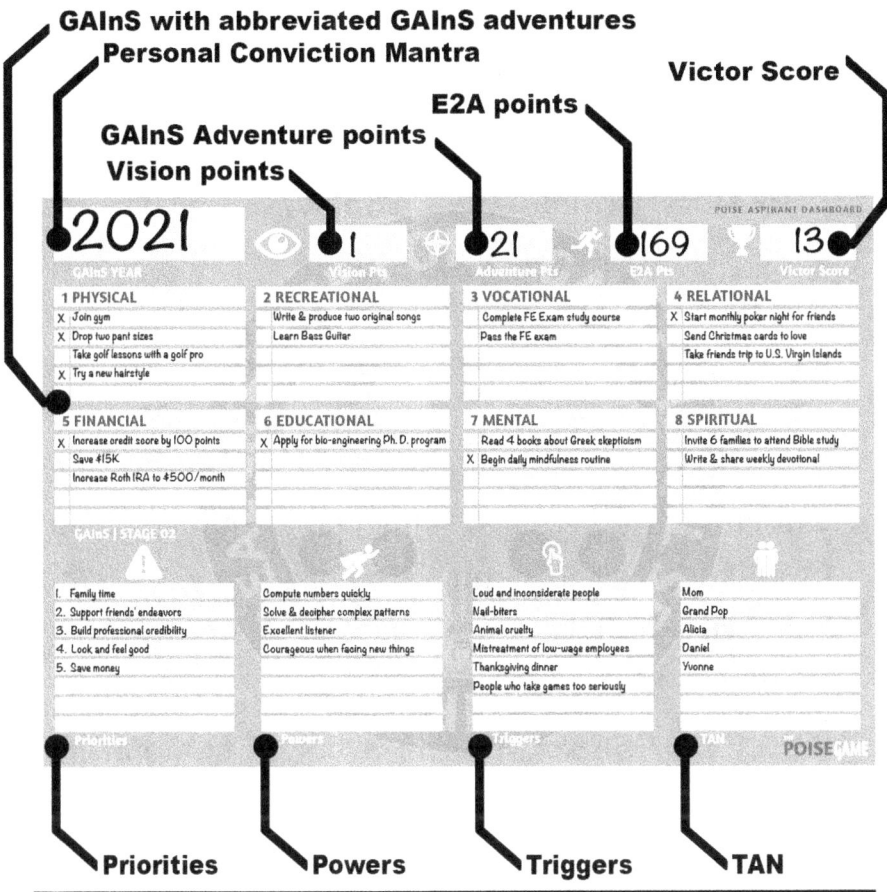

Vision Board | Back Side

to keep you accountable to your declarations, your values, and your vision. You may have several people in your network, but here you should select ones who you want to highlight. If you prefer to leave this section blank, then that's fine, but ensure that doesn't mean you don't have TAN members because your TAN is an important tool that enables your progress toward becoming your best self and living your best life.

Additional Sheets

• ***GAInS Adventure Sheet.*** This is the sheet where the long format for the GAInS Adventures are listed in accordance with the SMART Adventure-setting Method.

• ***T2D List sheet.*** This is a blank sheet. You can make copies of it to use at your leisure each time you make the T2D List. This is a formatted sheet to make creating your T2D Lists easy, but you can write your lists anywhere that's convenient for you.

• ***E2A List sheet.*** This is a list of custom and generic E2As. As you think of them, you can write them here to have a pool of choices in the event you're searching for a productive activity.

These are the majority of the tools that you must produce to play The Poise Game. There is a direct and positive correlation between the quality of your gameplay and the quality and quantity of effort you invest in producing your tools.

These examples of The Poise Game Tools can also be found in the back of the book in the section called 'The Poise Game Tools.'

Free templates can be downloaded at www.poisegame.com.

The tools listed in this chapter are designed to allow you to play the game autonomously, but the fact of the matter is that you are better when you have a team you can trust, especially in times of need.

In the next chapter, you will learn the importance of building your team and then learn how to assemble and manage it.

Your Team

"Your truest friends are the ones who will stand by you in your darkest moments—because they're willing to brave the shadows with you—and in your greatest moments—because they're not afraid to let you shine."

Nicole Yatsonsky

You've assembled a box of tools that are perfectly suited for you to help you realize your vision of becoming your best self and living your best life.

There is one more tool to complete your set, and that tool is your team—your Trusted Accountability Network.

The Trusted Accountability Network, or TAN, is a critical component to supporting you on your journey and consists of the important people you know who are honest, insightful, trustworthy, industrious, loyal and, assuredly, have your best interests at heart. Your TAN includes people who have vested interests in your success and will maintain your confidence, serving as encouraging partners through the highs, lows, and everything in-between.

Your TAN will afford you the fullest benefit of accountability and support during the effort to complete E2As as you develop greater ability to demonstrate poise. Your TAN includes people such as your significant other, friends, and family members who can help you complete E2As and GAInS Adventures, and encourage you when you find yourself needing support.

You should notify your TAN when you experience the joys of playing The Poise Game. These include, but aren't limited to, completing an aspect of your Vision, an annual GAInS, a GAInS Adventure, and notable E2As. Give your TAN the opportunity to share in your excitement. It's possible that your successes will serve as an inspiration.

You should also contact your TAN when you are experiencing mental obstacles or you have a series of undesirable outcomes that negatively impact your spirits. The people who care about you feel great honor when you entrust them with your difficulties because that means you believe that they have the power to do something about them. Maybe they can make the problem go away or maybe they can help you see it differently. In either case, you sharing your challenges with your TAN gives the members purpose and utility.

Establishing Your TAN

Being that it is a sacred appointment to place a person in your TAN, I recommend you inform each member selected. Many people don't realize how much they mean to you, so, at a minimum, this may be an opportunity to express to your selected TAN members how much and what they mean to you.

It's important that you explain to your TAN members what functions accompany their appointment. Be prepared for a range of responses. Perhaps they continue being the partner, friend, and loved one who they've always been. That makes it easy. The only adjustments may be that it takes some time for them to assimilate to some of The Poise Game lingo.

In other cases, this appointment may come with some surprising resistance.

Perhaps a selected TAN member is honored, but expresses that he or she isn't comfortable with the seemingly formalized responsibility.

Allow yourself the freedom to experience whatever emotions result from that resistance.

If you want to keep the person as a TAN member in a passive capacity, then explain that to him or her, highlighting how much it would mean to you and how much you would respect his or her wishes to only engage when it's a serious event or one that only he or she could perceivably provide support.

If the prospective TAN member insists upon rejecting the appointment, then express your gratitude for his or her honesty.

Believe it or not, this is a gift to you. You now know that you should look elsewhere for support regarding matters of importance to you.

TAN Maintenance

There's another reason you should contact your TAN.

You must make a habit of contacting your TAN members simply because they are special to you.

How many times have you heard the unfortunate tale of a loved one dying and some of the survivors expressing grief, not about the passing, but about the fact that they never told that person how they felt?

As a demonstration of your poise, incorporate making a regular call or sending the members of your TAN an email, a text, social media message, or an audio or video recorded message. If you're interested in really giving someone a pleasant surprise, write a handwritten letter and send it in the mail. That's a sure way to express your appreciation for their love, loyalty and friendship. You can perform unsolicited gestures directly for them that you know are the things they appreciate, but would rarely request. Give tokens of appreciation on their behalf to people, organizations, and causes that matter to them.

While it's important that your TAN members meet your specific qualifications and are available when you call, it's also imperative that you conduct frequent maintenance of your team. You must nurture it. Provide nourishment and sustenance that allows it to be ready and capable in the days when you must rely upon it to possibly dig you out of the darkness, and on those special days when your vision becomes reality.

TAN Operative Qualities

The TAN is a tool that you want to use if you're serious about playing The Poise Game. But it comes with some inherent risks that you should be prepared to experience. It's similar to any tool in the toolbox as it has great utility, but you should always exercise caution and vigilance because the tools have the potential of hurting you.

Trusted
Must be reliable with information you share and regarding information that impacts your well-being

Accountability
Must be accountable to your highest ideals that align with your vision

Network
Must be accessible and responsive to your efforts to connect

TAN Operative Qualities

You must ensure that your team is personally vetted and comprises individuals who know your vision and care to help you successfully achieve it. The risks associated with your TAN are related to members failing to adhere to the operative functions.

Trust is the first operative word in TAN. That's why the first risk associated with your TAN is that a member violates your trust.

You must be able to rely on your TAN members with personal and private information that is on a need-to-know basis and only the people with whom you directly share it have a need to know.

If a member of your TAN discloses trusted information, I believe it's fair for you to practice your poise by expressing your sentiments. This will be a situation where you will likely experience hurt, betrayal, embarrassment, disappointment and anger.

Depending upon your triggers, this also may be an incident wherein you must intercept your developed instinct of self-preservation that leads to destructive retaliatory behaviors.

You should know that it's okay to allow yourself the freedom to express your emotions, but those emotions are for your hurts. There is seldom an occasion where you can effectively share the hurt you experience that was contributed to by another.

Although the other person may conceptually understand your sentiments, there are few people with empathic abilities developed sufficiently to truly experience it the way you do. And even those who have the ability would need to be of the mindset that they desire to share what may be a painful and troublesome experience.

Treat this situation with gratitude to practice your poise, understanding that only you can control what you convey, but you cannot control how the other person responds. You must make a choice to prioritize either effective communication or freedom of expression during your engagement, and be accepting of the outcomes that may result from each, given the person with whom you are engaging.

Communicate your observations to your TAN member as clearly as possible, underscoring that sharing your private information with others is not acceptable. Allow him or her to provide an explanation if you desire to hear one. I recommend that you choose to forgo the explanation because no explanation will suffice for the behavior. Furthermore, listening to what amounts to a justification for the unwarranted behavior creates added risks that you become triggered by the recounting of the events surrounding your confidence being betrayed.

You must make a decision to maintain this person as a member of your TAN. The choice is entirely up to you, but if you choose to keep this person on your TAN, you should forgive the betrayal and practice restraint when feelings of retaliation and embitterment attempt to express themselves toward him or her. If these feelings become incapacitating or difficult to manage in context of your priorities, then you should remove the person from your TAN. Also, if he or she is confrontational or dismissive, then he or she doesn't meet the basic qualifications of the appointment and should, for the sake of your vision and your relationship, be removed from your TAN.

The second operative word in the TAN is 'accountability.' Therefore, the second risk is that a member of your TAN doesn't agree with your aims. This member is not accountable to your vision.

There will be occasions where members of your TAN disagree with an aspect of your vision, a GAInS Adventure, or what you perceive as E2As. You will want to assess whether the disagreement is a healthy form of devil's advocacy, but ultimately the support is constructive and encouraging or if it is criticism for criticism's sake that lacks substantive direction and is discouraging.

If it's the former, then I recommend you keep that member as part of your team. If it's the latter, then you should strongly consider whether the person should remain as a TAN member. It's okay for the person to be a cherished loved one and not have him or her as a member of your TAN. Your TAN members should be keeping you accountable to something and that something is your vision and the GAInS Adventures and E2As that support it. If that's not happening, then he or she doesn't meet the basic qualifications of the appointment and should, for the sake of your vision and your relationship, be removed from your TAN.

If you're paying attention, then you realize that 'network' is the third operative word in TAN. That means the third risk is that a member of your TAN is unavailable or consistently unwilling to share in your happiness or offer counsel, aid, and comfort in your times of need. This member is not an accessible member of your network.

Since you notified this individual that he or she was a member of a select group of special people in your life, I believe it's fair for you to practice your poise by expressing your sentiments regarding his or her unavailability. It's okay to allow yourself the freedom to express your emotions, but you must be aware that you cannot control how the other person will respond. Therefore, you want to prioritize either effective communication or freedom of expression during your engagement with the respective TAN member, and understand the probable outcomes that may result from each, given the person with whom you are engaging.

I also recommend that you take note of the situations that may be occurring in your TAN member's life. It's possible that he or she is experiencing difficulties or changes that are contributing to the behavior you're observing. As an Aspirant, you should exercise restraint and compassion for his or her situation, knowing that if it were you, then you would hope that you could at least count on the people who care for you to extend you some leniency.

If your inquiry to that TAN member's situation reveals that there isn't a notable reason for the observed behavior toward you, then you should communicate your observations to the TAN member, underscoring your desire to understand which occasions you can effectively engage with him or her. If he or she is confrontational or dismissive, then he or she doesn't meet the basic qualifications of the appointment and should, for the sake of your vision and your relationship, be removed from your TAN.

Assessing Your TAN

Each time you engage your TAN members, whether for reasons of support or for you to conduct your maintenance, you should conduct an assessment. You're paying attention to responsiveness, tone, sentiments, interest, changes in values and changes in loyalties. If you observe any notable changes, determine if it's something you believe should be addressed immediately through inquiry or if it's something that you prefer to watch.

Understand that your TAN may transform as you advance in poise level and achieve more vision points. This is not a problem and it doesn't mean that any member of your TAN did something wrong. There is a natural life cycle that varies based on the differing connection points you share with the individuals on your TAN. Some will be your TAN members for life. Some will be TAN members for decades. Some will be TAN members for a year or a few seasons. Any of these is okay.

Give yourself the freedom to appreciate their contributions to your life and, if you're following the guidance I'm providing, your contributions to their lives.

After reading the risks associated with having a TAN, keeping your list with zero members may sound appealing. However, there is a risk with going solo as well.

At some point you will inevitably require another person in some form or fashion. This is okay. And this is why the TAN exists. Some of the most superficial reasons for having a TAN, such as a person congratulating you on your accomplishment of an E2A, may seem inconsequential until you realize you long for it.

It's like drinking water when you're in the heat. As long as you take a few sips throughout the day, then you'll be fine.

You likely won't experience thirst nor will you experience the pangs of heat exhaustion. But if you wait until you're thirsty to drink, then it's too late. Suddenly a throbbing headache follows, your skin feels clammy, and your thirst for water becomes insatiable but no amount seems to quench it.

Your TAN is as essential to your vision as water is to your health.

The benefits of the TAN are outlined in its definition. It is a person or group of people who you can trust, who are willing to hold you accountable to your vision, and who will be available when you seek to engage. While having several members in your TAN could be useful, if you have one quality person, that's all you may need.

At this point, you may feel like you have been involved in a long-term research project. Taking the time to contemplate and then produce the Poise Game tools was a significant effort. Now that you know how to derive your TAN, you have completed the construction of your tools so your focus will shift from the tools of the game to the methods.

In the forthcoming chapters you will learn The Poise Game methods that will help to set the mental conditions that are required to most effectively wield these tools. Some of the methods will sound familiar, so it will be a reminder in the context of the game. Some may be foreign; but all of them bring the utility necessary to give you the poise you need to cause your vision to manifest. These may not require as much writing and fabricating, but the thinking energy requirements may match or exceed what was asked from you during your toolmaking.

Can you play the Poise Game and make steady progress toward your vision without implementing the prescribed methods in this book?

Perhaps.

But if you were successfully doing that already, then why are you reading this book?

I'm guessing for a friend, right?

Then tell your friend to lace-up those shoes because we're about to get to what may be the hardest work yet—renewing your mind.

Your Choice

"A life lived by choice is a life of conscious action. A life lived by chance is a life of unconscious reaction."

Neale Donald Walsch

You always have a choice.

There are few occasions in which you cannot determine your own response to your situation. That doesn't mean that the fact that you have a choice means it's easy or even something you desire or are willing to do. But your choice is always yours.

Everything you've learned about the Poise Game up until now has been leading you to this moment. Earlier I told you that, since you began reading this book, you are now playing the game. You are an Aspirant.

That choice is beyond you. But what remains is your decision regarding the way you plan to play the game. Fundamentally, the manner in which you play the Poise Game is tantamount to who you are and the way you live.

That is why the next decision you make is extremely important. Do you choose to be a victor of choice or a victim of circumstance?

The answer seems obvious, but if you take an assessment of the people you encounter on a daily basis at school, work, on the news, even when you're vacationing, there seems to be an air of defeatism when it comes to the events that take place in our lives and their associated outcomes.

This victim of circumstance worldview subtly reinforces itself as it's ingrained in the everyday language you hear. Think about common statements that sound inconsequential but are declarations of faith because the speaker and the listener believe the words to be true. For instance, I'm sure you've said or heard someone say, "He makes me angry!" or "the traffic jam caused me to be late." Or "work is stressing me out." These statements might contain elements of truth, but they all convey something less apparent.

Be the Subject Rather Than the Object

I'm going to take you back to your fifth grade

English Composition lessons for a moment. In these sentences, the person who is speaking makes someone or something other than him or herself the subject of the sentence. The subject is the person or thing that takes action in the sentence. That means you as the speaker take the place of the object being acted upon when you speak that way.

When you are a victor of choice you are the subject of your sentences because you recognize your power to make deliberate decisions. You make things happen instead of things happening to make you.

When you are a victim of circumstance you are the object of your sentences because you relinquish your authority to make deliberate decisions. Things happen to you instead of you making them happen.

There are certainly a few questions that you may have about becoming a victor of choice.

For instance, what is the difference between choice and circumstance?

Choice is the autonomous, self-determined demonstration of your executive function to select, reject, or modify options within an observed range. Circumstance is a condition connected to your experience of an event, action, or outcome. The former implies control. The latter implies subjugation.

In The Poise Game, you want to be the victor of choice. The victor of choice is an Aspirant who acknowledges the range of options within his or her perceptual field, then confidently and deliberately chooses those which align most with his or her vision.

When you are a victor of choice, you know these three things: First, you know that your current perspective is your choice. Oftentimes, people have the tendency to believe their perspective is something given to them. As a victor of choice, you subscribe to the idea that, while shaped by an infinite amount of inputs, including your DNA, experiences and mindset, your perspective only exists as it does because you choose to keep it as it is.

Second, as a victor you know that your perspective shapes the options you believe you have. You are aware that the menu of decisions you consider are limited to your current worldview. This isn't wrong. It's simply an acknowledgment that if you are dissatisfied with the options available, then you are the one who must do something about it.

That leads to the third thing victors know. You know you can change your perspective. You know that it is temporarily fixed because you choose to keep it that way to create a sense of consistency and minimize disruptive variables in your perceptual plane. The moment you determine that your current perspective doesn't serve your best interests because your range of options do not sufficiently lead to desirable outcomes, then you alone have

> From this point forward, I accept responsibility for all my life's experiences—past, present and future.
>
> I may not control everything that I encounter, but I control its impact upon me.
>
> My perspective is the lens from which I perceive the world. It's my creation. It shapes what I believe are my options. Based upon it, I will make the best possible decisions.
>
> If I decide to expand my purview, then I can change it whenever I choose.
>
> The power of choice is mine, and no one and nothing can take it from me, unless I relinquish it.
>
> But I won't because as a victor, I am charged with the mandate to deliberately progress toward my highest ideals.
>
> This task requires self-control, which I embody through my poise. It is not a task that I can delegate.
>
> **THE POISE GAME**   I am the champion of my vision.
>
> I am a victor of choice.

Victor of Choice Pledge

the ability to change it.

With this knowledge, you also realize that as your worldview transforms, your options will expand proportionately so you seek opportunities to obtain knowledge. Knowledge is the substance of the perceptual field. With an increase in knowledge you are able to place it within context of your current experiences and intellect to widen the limits of your options.

When I'm referring to choice. Let me be clearer: As a victor of choice, you recognize your experience is directly attributable to your deliberate choices of commission and omission.

A choice of commission is an action that was performed. A choice of omission is an action that was not performed. In either case, as the victor you accept responsibility for the outcomes that occur as a result of your choices.

You want to avoid becoming a victim of circumstance. A victim of circumstance is a person who limits the range of options within his or her perceptual field, then assigns responsibility for making choices to another person, the environment or the cosmos, even if the choice is contrary to his or her vision.

When you are a victim of circumstance, you believe these three things: First, you believe that your current perspective is not your choice. You believe, like many others you know, that your perspective was something given to you. You subscribe to the idea that your perspective is the direct result of meaningful inputs, especially the hereditary components and your experiences. Your perspective is the direct product of these and many other inputs and is fixed.

Second, as a victim you believe that others and the divine shape and determine the quality and quantity of options you have. You don't believe you have many options, if any at all. And, of the available options, most are incongruent with your ideals. You feel it's not fair, but there's not much you can do. If you are dissatisfied with the options available, then you petition, plead with, and ultimately blame the external forces acting upon your situation.

Third, as a victim you believe you can't change your perception. In fact, it's not a concept or idea that ever crossed your mind. Because it was given to you and shaped by external forces, you treat it as a cherished possession. Your worldview is set and you believe in the idea of its fixed state so much that you are willing to fight to hold onto it. Even though it doesn't serve your desires, it's familiar. There's comfort in familiarity. Since you don't feel you have any good options, you'd rather keep a bad one that's familiar. You're caught in a perceptual Stockholm Syndrome. You believe your choices are appropriate responses given the environment you are forced to exist within so you are not fully responsible for them.

Two Perspectives: Victor Versus Victim

One thing should be clear: there are things that occur that are beyond your direct control. Those things bear the weight of the collective experiences and desires of countless people to bring them to fruition.

As an Aspirant and a victor, you treat all situations you experience in the same way. You consider them in context of your perceptual plane. You determine your available options. You choose one of the options or, if none of the available options are sufficient, you expand your perceptual plane to reveal additional options. Once you observe an option that aligns with your vision, you choose it. You will encounter situations that are not what you would consciously desire. And as a victor, you are grateful that you have the ability to shape even the most tragic situations into the most triumphant celebrations.

Another point that should be stated is that the characterizations I make about victims of circumstance is not an attack against you or anyone else who is suffering or has suffered detestable abuse at the hands of others. The list of heinous acts people do to others is real—sexual assault and harassment, child molestation, human-trafficking, domestic violence, stalking, bullying, racism, robbery and murder.

It is out of the dignity and respect I have for you and anyone who has experienced these appalling acts that I offer a way to regain and claim the power that you may believe was stolen from you. That is a ruse. Despite the severity of the abuse you experienced, your light, though it may be dim, still shines.

I'm sure the people who encourage you to identify as a victim of one of the above instances do so with good intentions. Perhaps they believe that it's a part of your healing and will help you to move forward. The challenge is that when you choose the role of a victim of circumstance, then you must play that role. I understand that you may have a desire to describe yourself as a victim to stand in solidarity with others who have shared your pains. Once again, in order to assume that role, you must adopt its characteristics.

The characteristics of a victim of circumstance are assuredly incongruent with you as an Aspirant playing the Poise Game. Your efforts to progress toward becoming your best self and living your best life will be disrupted by the fundamental attribute of the victim of circumstance—as a victim, you are not in control. And if you have no self-control, then you fail to demonstrate poise that leads to productive decisions relating to your highest ideals about yourself and your life.

Hopefully, at this point the reason why you should choose to be a victor of choice is apparent. But if it isn't, then consider this. You basically have the option to be a champion of all of your causes. You are free to make decisions, hold fast to your proclivities and change your mind if those decisions are consistent with your vision. You are free from needing to judge other people's actions and contributions to your progress because you respect their freewill to do what they desire to do as much as you appreciate your own.

One more thing.

You are free to choose not to be the victor, but that choice also means you choose not to win.

Even if you go through the functional steps of playing the Poise Game, without the victor perspective, you will not be able to fully develop your poise ability because you believe other factors have the control. If you don't eventually choose the victor perspective, then your small wins of completing E2As will begin to lose value and, ultimately, if you face hardship, you will experience your vision as an indictment based upon your ineptitude, rather than a motivation based upon your potential.

Victor of Choice Pledge

If you realized the prudence in choosing to be a victor of choice, then you're probably wondering what your next step should be. How do you become a victor of choice?

The answer is simple.

Find a mirror. Look yourself in the eyes and recite the following Victor of Choice Pledge:

> *From this point forward, I accept responsibility for all my life's experiences—*

past, present and future.

I may not control everything that I encounter, but I control its impact upon me.

My perspective is the lens from which I perceive the world. It's my creation. It shapes what I believe are my options. Based upon it, I will make the best possible decisions.

If I decide to expand my purview, then I can change it whenever I choose.

The power of choice is mine, and no one and nothing can take it from me, unless I relinquish it.

But I won't because as a victor, I am charged with the mandate to deliberately progress toward my highest ideals.

This task requires self-control, which I embody through my poise. It is not a task that I can delegate.

I am the champion of my vision.

I am a victor of choice.

If you recited this pledge, then congratulations

for taking another step toward becoming your best self and living your best life.

As a symbol of your choice, I recommend you grab your Poise Deck, shuffle it and draw a card until you find an E2A you'd like to do, and then complete it.

If you don't have your Poise Deck ready, then that's okay, you can do anything or do nothing.

Either way, it's your choice.

Victor in Practice

Even though you accept the call to become a victor of choice, there will be times that challenge your commitment to your principles. In those moments, the displeasure you sense will seek solace through blaming others, taking offense and feeling hopelessness.

You must guard yourself against the urges that draw you into the abyss where you lay aside your power and succumb to the delusion that someone or something else is the cause of your undesirable experience.

If you sense your mind searching for a name to accuse, provide your name instead. While the cause of your troubles may be external, as a victor, you refuse to dignify anyone or anything with the honor of determining the quality of your experience.

If you begin to sense that you are taking offense to something that is occurring, take a deep breath. Take a few if one isn't enough. Then forgive the offender. To be offended requires effort on your part. That's why it is called taking offense. If you forgive the offender, then there is no requirement for your offensive that you are preparing. You may feel like forgiving the offender may be easier said than done, but as a victor of choice, you will weigh the cost of responding to the offense any other way and realize it's not worth the value of your time.

If you sense that you are feeling ashamed or embarrassed about something you did, something you're doing, or an observable aspect of your character or your world, find where the energy relating to the shame is physically located in your body.

You may need to take a moment to find it.

Consider your Five As exercise where you used aesthetics, attitudes, activities, affiliations and accomplishments to describe your best self.

Reflect upon the environmental factors, including atmosphere, domicile, topography, neighborhood, residence and climate that helped you describe your best life.

Once you find that energy, identify what it is that you are attributing to the feeling of shame. Take command of that energy and use it to resolve your shame. If it's a past behavior that you don't intend to do again, then admit to yourself that you did it. Admit that you made that choice at that time to behave that way. And acknowledge that you are making a choice at this time to behave differently and in a more productive way. Express gratitude for the insight that shameful decision provides you today. Forgive yourself for the harm it caused you and others.

If it's something you're currently doing, then stop doing it immediately. Now it's technically in the past so you can address it the same way you address past unproductive behavior. If it's something about your aesthetics, attitude or aspirations, determine if you're willing to change the thing that you're attributing to your shame. If you are, then envision yourself with this item in its ideal state and add it to your Vision Board and GAInS, if it's not already reflected.

Reframe your perspective to understand yourself as a work in progress. A homebuilder isn't ashamed when he only has the foundation laid or when the home only has the framing erected. These are natural progressions in the process of building the home. In the same way, you can appreciate your own process and shift your energy from shame to determination to see it through to the end.

If you don't intend to change the items you believe you are ashamed about, then you are likely not ashamed about them, but ashamed that your current conditions are incongruent with them. In this case, you should apply the same perspective shift, to acknowledge you're a person under construction. In fact, you are constructing the person you choose to be and the life you choose to live right now. Your energy reallocated toward your determination will transform shame into positive and productive momentum. Spend any remaining energy in gratitude that you recognize the power of your choice.

If you sense a feeling of hopelessness setting in upon you, you must do three things without hesitation.

First, perform a kind act for a person who is not a loved one. Be creative. You could pay the grocery bill for the family behind you in line. You could offer to mow your neighbor's lawn. Or if you are struggling to find someone, you could always pick up trash along the side of the road or at your local park.

Second, call at least one loved one and tell him or her how grateful you are for the love he or she gives you. If that call gives you a spark of joy, then make another one. You can make as many as you want, but you only need to make one call.

Third, play at least one stage of the Poise Game. If you want to be quick you can go straight to stage four, the Poise Deck. But if you have time, I recommend beginning at stage one and working your way through the graduated poise pattern.

The key is that you choose to complete at least one E2A. If you're motivated, then you can do one per stage. If not, then just do one. Once you've completed these three things, take the time to reflect upon the hope you give, the hope you receive, and the hope to come. Just like when you have light, there is no darkness. When you have hope, there is no hopelessness.

One of the notable things about combating your urges to become a victim of circumstance is that when you follow the prescribed guidance above and successfully thwart the call to relinquish your power, you earn a Victor point. These are reflected on your Poise Aspirant Dashboard and are one of the pieces of information that carry over from dashboard to dashboard as you progress through the years.

Your Victor points are similar to a sniper's kill count. I don't believe you should make a habit of boasting, but your Victor points are where I think you should make an exception. Every time you make a deliberate decision to be a victor, despite the various reasons that may present themselves to you as justification for playing the victim, you make significant progress toward achieving your vision because by doing so you improve your ability to demonstrate poise.

Maintaining your stature as a victor of choice is the prerequisite to the following methods in the forthcoming chapters. Now that you recognize your power is based upon your ability to choose, in the next chapter you will learn how to employ your power through your thoughts, emotions, words and deeds. For it is through the wielding of your power that you can be, do, and have.

Your Mindset

"Once you make a decision, the universe conspires to make it happen."

Ralph Waldo Emerson

Your mindset represents your dexterity, which enables you to employ your creative powers, including thoughts, emotions, words and deeds.

After you accept the role of the victor, you then must adopt the capabilities of one. As an Aspirant, you subscribe to the eternal triad that underscores life—Be-Do-Have. The components of this triad have harmonious relationships where discord is impossible. It is the truest picture of who you are, what you do, and what you have.

The first component is to "Be."

Saying "I am" is a declaration of faith that focuses your manifesting energy on your beingness. When you assert that something "is", you are setting the powers in motion to manifest exactly what you declare. If you "be" something, that means your essence and attributes converge to make you exactly who you say you are.

The second component is to "Do."

Your actions are purposeful and abide according to the law of reciprocity, which states that you reap what you sow. Some people look at it in the light of what Hindus call Karma—an eternal cycle of cause and effect.

Others relate it to a Judeo-Christian maxim that says do to others what you would have them do to you. The key to understanding your actions is that what you do determines who you are because who you are determines what you do.

The third component of the triad is to "Have."

Your possessions and resources are not mere contrivances, they also have utility because they are indicators. It is similar to the age-old question: which came first, the chicken or the egg?

In the case of what you have, it is related to who you are and what you do. In fact, it is evidence that you are who you are and you do what you do. This is because to have the things you possess, those things are conditional based upon who you are and what you do.

The triad exists in perfect harmony because you cannot be if you don't have that which is necessary for you to be, and you cannot do if you don't have that which is necessary for you to do. In order for you to be and to do, you must have.

You will use the eternal triad as a tool to calibrate your efforts. When you assess your "Be, Do, and Have," if what emerges is not on the path to your vision, then you should reconsider the merits of your vision or adjust your thoughts, emotions, words and deeds to match your vision.

Speaking of which, now we'll discuss your weapons of your Aspirant mindset.

Four-Pronged Conveyance Faculties

One of the things that makes humans different from other sentient beings on earth is our metacognitive ability. Metacognition is the ability to think about thinking. With the capacity for analyzing your own thoughts from an external observer's purview, you are able to identify inefficiencies and unproductive logical fallacies, and make choices to adjust your thinking to align with your desires.

Until now, you've probably noted that I keep

emphasizing the importance of your thoughts, emotions, words and deeds. Now let me give them a name that describes what they are to you as an Aspirant. They are your four-pronged conveyance faculties. Through the employment of these faculties, you demonstrate your highest executive function of self-control.

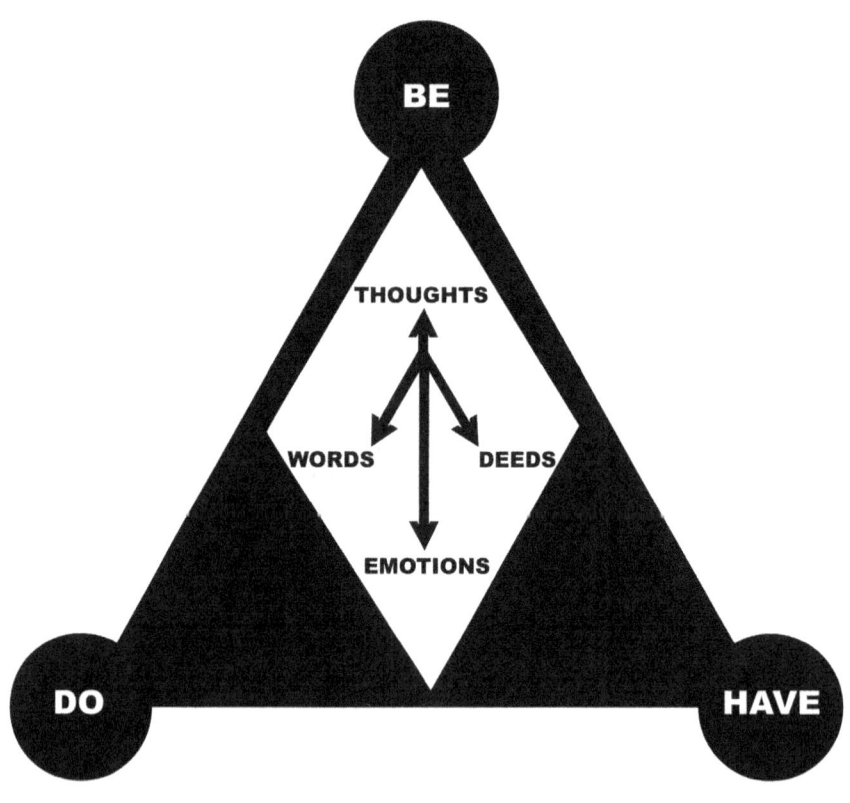

Eternal Triad & Four-pronged Conveyance Faculties

The first prong of your conveyance faculties is your thoughts. Your thoughts are a separate prong but also provide complementary assistance to the other faculties. If you are determined to make a deliberate choice, then it starts with your thoughts.

Now if you consider the idea of your thoughts, you realize that thoughts are the byproduct of some activity. The activity that produces thought is thinking; therefore, to have thoughts you must think. Thinking can be initiated involuntarily, but the moment you are conscious or aware of your thoughts, you are able to control them.

As an Aspirant, you regularly use metacognition to perform a mental quality assurance and quality control check.

Quality assurance aims to ensure you are practicing productive thinking, which should result in productive thoughts. Quality control aims to assess your thoughts, identify those that are unproductive, and fix them before they lead to subsequent unproductive activities.

The very act of thinking is the beginning of the creative process. It's like turning on the machines and preparing the materials. The longer the thought is held and nurtured, the more power and resources it receives.

The risk to you is that thoughts don't selectively distinguish between what is productive and unproductive.

Thoughts operate under the presumption that if you hold them in your mind, then you intend for them to manifest.

What's fortunate is that it is equally easy to produce productive thoughts as it is to produce unproductive ones. If you find yourself in a situation in which you must react to the manifestations of your own unproductive thoughts, then accept the situation with gratitude for the evidence of your creative power, then adjust your thinking to produce and maintain productive thoughts.

Thoughts are one of the two conveyance faculties that transits through internal pathways. The other is emotions.

The second prong of your conveyance faculties is your emotions. Your emotions seem like automatic responses to your thoughts and external inputs; however, that's not the entire story. While the flash-to-bang for emotions typically occurs within a blink of an eye, the key to managing your emotions is two-part. Before we discuss the two parts, if your emotions sufficiently align with your vision concerning who you choose to be, what you choose to do, and what you choose to have, then this section will simply be for your use, given your situation changes. Otherwise keep emoting effectively.

So the first thing you must do to manage your emotions is to sensitize your ability to find the point of origin for your emotions. This is important because, like an investigator, you can determine the emotional trigger from the point of its origin.

Just as thoughts are the byproduct of thinking, emotions are the byproduct of emoting. The problem is that we tend to only observe the emotionally triggering event and the subsequent emotions. In between there includes thinking that produces thoughts and thoughts that initiate energy for you to emote.

You may spend a lifetime attempting to decipher the exact point when your thoughts transition to emoting activity, and the good thing is that won't be necessary. As I stated before, your thoughts are complementary to the other conveyance faculties. In this case, you will recognize your thoughts, analyze them to determine if they are productive, and if not, then you must change them accordingly.

Now this first part for managing your emotions works when you are conscious of your thoughts that precipitate the emotions. The second part of managing your emotions will be familiar because it involves identifying your triggers and creating a mechanism for assessing if the subsequent emotions are consistent with your broader interests. If it isn't, then you adjust your thinking, which will produce thoughts that lead to emotions that align with your vision. To review my method for addressing triggers, go back to chapter six where it discusses triggers in the Poise Aspirant Dashboard.

The third prong of your conveyance faculties is words. Your words are a creative action that magnifies the power of your thoughts to compel that which is spoken into existence. Words have the unique ability to bless and to curse. For this reason, you should be mindful to use words carefully because once uttered, the energy they project cannot be undone. You can attempt to mitigate the effects, but more than likely, if your words are unproductive, you will need to prepare to address the fruit of your own making.

Similar to how thoughts are the product of thinking and emotions the product of emoting, words are the product of speaking.

The clever thing about words, unlike thoughts and emotions, is that they can contain layers of meaning to those who hear them.

As an Aspirant, you are deliberate about the surface text and subtext of your spoken conveyances. You understand the potential for dispatching efforts that conflict with each other from the words you say. You appreciate the relationship between your thoughts and your words and employ your ability to speak in a way that aligns with what you envision.

Words are also the easiest to employ because you don't have to have tangible evidence of them to speak them. The only thing necessary for your words to transmit power is faith that they are true.

This can generate thoughts that lead to emotions and then more words and deeds. Words represent one of the two conveyance faculties that transits through external pathways.

The other is deeds.

The fourth prong of the conveyance faculties is deeds. Deeds are your physical actions, excluding speaking.

Your actions are the most dependent conveyance faculty because they rely upon your thoughts, emotions, and sometimes your words to generate the inertia to act. Your actions also have the ability to generate thoughts, emotions and words because of the tangible results that they produce. For example, if you desire to be a writer, but aren't one yet, then you can write, and by doing so you have evidence that suggests you are becoming a writer because writing is what writers do.

You can use your deeds to cultivate the productive thoughts and emotions that then project the confidence that you can be a writer.

In this way, if you aren't yet what you aspire to be, then do the things you would do if you were, and then you become exactly who you choose to be because of what you do.

What happens is that the deeds send a signal that produces related thoughts, then those thoughts create emotions and the emotions are accompanied by words that produce additional deeds.

If you desire to be a writer, then write, and do the other things a writer does. If you desire anything, then align your deeds accordingly and your desires will come to fruition. To have thoughts you must think, to have emotions, you must emote, to have words you must speak, and to have deeds you must act.

Deeds are the tangible representation of the law of cause and effect. You can visibly see that you reap what you sow.

Six Disciplines of an Aspirant

It took me over a decade to fully understand the benefits of taking the time to establish a productive mindset for myself.

I'm going to save you some time by sharing with you the situation that nudged me into certainty regarding the functional utility and qualitative value of your conveyance faculties.

One evening I was meditating. I remember concentrating on my breaths and giving myself the freedom to explore various thoughts. Thoughts that I normally brush aside because they seemed frivolous or irrelevant were allowed to move across the domain of my mind. That's when a thought caught my attention. I followed it and in doing so I was given a strong urge to read some of the classic novels that were part of the academic requirements from when I was a teenager.

I recalled that during high school I used a combination of skimming techniques and Cliff's Notes for essays and exams, then I'd dump the

1 Do your homework
2 Be compassionate
3 Ask for help
4 Forgive
5 Project confidence & humility
6 Have integrity

Six Disciplines for Developing Mindset

information and proceed to the next assignment on the agenda. I sensed that while this approach may earn you "As" in school, it can cause you to get "Fs" in some key lessons of life.

I needed to explore these texts to find nuggets of wisdom that I had missed as a youth.

So I responded to the impulse and began to read

several classics of literature—Great Expectations, Crime and Punishment, Herland, Sherlock Holmes, Lord of the Flies, The Most Dangerous Game, and Animal Farm to name a few.

As I suspected, I found some hidden gems that I missed as a kid.

It was in the novel Around the World in 80 Days by Jules Verne where I found the best example of effective application of the conveyance faculties.

The protagonist, Phileas Fogg, an Aspirant in all respects, completed several adventures on his way to achieving his vision. In the book, Fogg, a wealthy Englishman, makes a bet valued at $2.5 million that he could circumnavigate the world in exactly 80 days. Determined to be a man of his word, he sets out to accomplish this feat despite several deliberate efforts and undesirable mishaps creating obstacles in his path.

I'd like to point out that most of the poise methods were derived from similar situations like the one described. I've highlighted this one as an illustration of what's possible if you sensitize yourself and are open to learning from anything, even the things that may be unassuming.

By the way, if you haven't read the book, there

will be a few spoilers here. I still recommend you read it for yourself, but for expediency I've extracted the relevant lessons it highlights.

What's key for you is not that this fictional character had mastery of his thoughts, emotions, words and deeds, but what he did to develop his ability to manage them.

I discovered there are six disciplines you as an Aspirant must practice to develop your ability to manage and effectively apply your conveyance faculties.

1. Do your homework.

Phileas Fogg was well-versed in several disciplines because he took the time to study, challenge himself and embrace alternative methods. The knowledge he used to travel the globe was obtained before making his substantial bet. There's no doubt that his confidence was based upon the fact that he did his homework. He learned what worked for him, but understood that alternative approaches could also serve a purpose.

What is your homework? It's the information relating to your vision, your adventures and your activities. It's the knowledge that allows you to confidently make decisions that are in line with your priorities. Doing your homework will serve to refine and reinforce your conveyance faculties so when you encounter challenges, you will be resilient.

2. Be compassionate.

During his trip, Phileas Fogg traveled through India where he stumbled upon a procession for a human sacrifice of a young widow, Aouda. From an outside observer's point-of-view, her unfortunate situation was in direct conflict with his current goal.

Remember, it's the late 1800s. Availability of reliable modes of travel are rare and he's already on a tight timeline. Any deviations could cause him to lose the bet and ruin him financially.

As he considered what to do, the clock continued ticking. There was a lot of money on the line, but so was his integrity.

What does Fogg do? He creates a plan with his traveling party and rescues the girl. He demonstrated compassion.

While his companions were sure he should give up, Fogg refused to let external inputs negatively impact his thoughts.

Compassion isn't convenient. Compassion may cost some of your time and energy.

But when you see a need, you have the opportunity

to make a choice. If you practice keeping your thoughts hopeful, then the way to success reveals itself and you realize it's connected to you being compassionate.

3. Ask for help.

Along the way, obstacles attempted to thwart Fogg's progress. And though he was resolute in his belief that he could circumnavigate the world in 80 days, he was not above asking for help.

He wasn't afraid to ask questions that may reveal his ignorance.

You've heard the saying, "There's no such thing as a dumb question." Well, the dumb question is the question that doesn't get asked. You've probably experienced a situation where you were too concerned about others forming a negative perception of you so you didn't ask a question or seek the help you needed.

As an Aspirant, you're not afraid to ask for assistance because you are humble enough to prioritize progress over pride.

And when accepting assistance, Fogg did so remarkably. He treated it as a delegated task. And though he would delegate tasks liberally, he never delegated his responsibility. He knew that when you delegate your responsibility, you also relinquish your authority. And without authority you no longer have your power. You are at the mercy of another person's choices.

This is an unacceptable predicament for an Aspirant because an Aspirant is a victor of choice. You seek assistance in every prudent and expedient way. You are grateful for help when it's rendered. But you always reserve your responsibility to the outcomes because you never forget that any additional aid—poorly or well executed—impacts your vision.

4. Forgive.

When you've been wronged, it takes—everything—to forgive.

Phileas Fogg had to do this, too. His assistant had a penchant for making mistakes.

Let's just list a couple of his costly mistakes he made. He left the gas heater running in his room before departing on their travels. Remember this is expected to be at least an 80-day trip. Also, during their trip, he got high smoking opium, and caused Phileas Fogg to miss his trans-Pacific ship ride.

Forgiveness served as a lever that freed Phileas Fogg from the burden of managing his assistant's mistakes.

The poet and priest, George Herbert, fittingly stated, "He who cannot forgive breaks the bridge over which he himself must pass." Unforgiveness toward other people and toward yourself spawns anger, vengeance, malice and embitterment as you replay the circumstances in which you were wronged. And each time you replay them in your mind, you make them new and present so your unforgiveness throws more weight upon the pile. It becomes a weight that you believe you must carry and before you realize it, the load is unbearable.

When you forgive, you acknowledge your pain and you let it go. You release it so that it releases you. Your understanding of the implications of becoming embittered shows you how to acknowledge offenses that may come, address them productively and then move on.

5. Project confidence and humility.

Being as rich and smart as Phileas Fogg was didn't entitle him to oppress others.

Whether speaking with his melodramatic servant, the young maiden he rescued, or a disrespectful passenger on a train, he balanced confidence and humility.

Think highly of yourself. You are special, but this doesn't mean you should think of other people as less deserving of honor, dignity and respect.

And though you should think well of yourself, be careful not to become your own fanatic.

If you're not mindful of this, you can easily slip into the trap of self-worship that leads you to placing yourself on a pedestal from where you will eventually fall.

Simply put, don't buy your own trading cards and action figures.

But your confidence should be something you exude because you are grateful for it. True confidence comes with the knowledge of the truth. Your truth is the vision you have and the faith that it's manifesting with every moment that passes.

This is a gift that you hope others can experience.

Your humility matches your confidence. You exude humility because you recognize that, if it weren't for the divine, if it weren't for the series of fortunate circumstances that led you to your current state of enlightenment, then you would be like a person staggering through the dark in search for the light.

Like the sun and moon, your confidence and

humility are involved in a never-ending dance through time and space, bringing about the seasons of life.

You must develop a knack for blending self-assurance with modesty. Then you can demonstrate how your confidence can be perfectly complemented by humility.

6. Have integrity.

Phileas Fogg valued his word above everything.

On one occasion, he was on a trans-Atlantic ship and the fuel ran out. Phileas Fogg made a deal with the captain: "I'll pay you the ship's full price if you burn parts of it for fuel, and you can keep the hull."

This was significantly more than market value for the trip and the cost of the ship, but when the ship docked, he kept his word.

Fogg understood that his integrity represented the essence of who he chose to be and how he chose to live. You know integrity means that you keep your word and follow-through with your commitments, even if they are difficult.

Sometimes having integrity also means that you will need to respectfully dissolve relationships and commitments that do not match your values or lead to your vision. In doing so, you can confidently pay the cost of your decisions because your integrity remains intact. With your integrity, you have the fortitude to withstand any challenges you face and the mindset to see the beacon of light that draws you to achieve your highest ideals.

Your word is your bond.

Your mindset is key to you making productive decisions that allow you to become your best self and live your best life. You now recognize the eternal triad is a way to test yourself to see if your mindset is calibrated to your vision. If it's not, then you know how to develop your ability to have thoughts, emotions, words and deeds that align with who you choose to be and how you choose to live.

A strong mindset and knowing how to use it are prerequisites for the next method you will learn, which will ask you to identify what's most important to you and unabashedly apply your value toward it.

Your Priorities

*"Don't compromise yourself.
You're all you've got."*

Janis Joplin

If you were to see a person driving a car, eating a sandwich and speaking on the phone, this wouldn't alarm or surprise you because it's become the norm.

In this fast-paced world, there is a lot of emphasis placed on your ability to multitask.

The issue is that this type of normalized behavior, which may not be such a big deal in isolation, has transferred into your broader decision-making, causing you to feel as if you commit an infraction if you choose to do one thing at a time.

As an Aspirant, you subscribe to believe that in all things you must prioritize, otherwise you compromise the vision you seek to attain.

Perhaps you're thinking that certainly there are times when multitasking is okay.

We agree.

There will be times when you recognize that urgency is most important, which then makes it acceptable to do more than one task at a time. The point is not that multitasking isn't permitted or is wrong. The point is that you must prioritize how you use your conveyance faculties and any other resources at your disposal or else you accept a greater risk of not progressing on your path.

Priorities and Their Benefits

A priority is anything that you deem to be important that you give the value of your energy, time, space and resources. In the Poise Game, your priorities must align with your vision and your vision must align with your priorities.

You can apply your value toward something that is not a priority, but that is an example of unproductive thoughts, emotions, words, and deeds. If you discover that you are giving your value to something that isn't listed as a priority, either you should stop and reallocate your value or you should consider making it a priority.

In order for it to be one of your priorities, it must

align with your vision. So if you make something a priority that previously wasn't, then you do so with the understanding that you are updating your vision. I want you to know that this is okay as long as it's your choice. Your priorities belong to you and contribute toward your vision, which is you becoming your best self and living your best life.

There are countless benefits to you subscribing to a choice of prioritization, but I'll just share a few. The rest will be for your discovery once you apply the method.

By prioritizing, you are able to increase your focus.

The world presents you with a variety of unlimited options for just about every decision you encounter. The way you are engaged, you'd think everyone is a marketer with insights into your deepest cravings and tastes.

The ability to focus, to zero in on a few important things, makes weeding through the minutia possible.

You rid yourself of unnecessary distractions and disruptions because stuff that doesn't contribute to your aims doesn't register on your radar. You remove the guesswork and consider only feasible options that meet your needs.

The other benefit to prioritizing is that you can reduce your waste.

If you knew how much of your value was wasted due to you not efficiently and effectively prioritizing your efforts, then you would probably be extremely upset with yourself.

But this isn't a time for you to self-deprecate. It's a time for you to self-appreciate through self-control.

The way you do that is by applying your value that is your energy, time, place and resources toward that which is important to you.

When should you intentionally apply your value toward something that's not a priority?

Never.

There are no occasions where you should apply your value toward anything that doesn't align with your vision.

In the world of around eight billion people, there is surely someone else more suited to apply their value toward those things that fall outside of your priorities and your vision than you are. Step aside and let that person spend away while you reserve the balance of your value for something more suitable for your vision another day.

The third benefit to you setting a list of priorities is that you can increase your productivity.

In the business world, productivity signifies more for the bottom-line. In your world, the bottom-line is your vision to become your best self and live your best life. With a simple list of things that you select as most important to you, you can give your best and whole-hearted effort toward accomplishing them and anything related to them.

Imagine a situation where you knew no matter what you did, it means you're one step closer to winning your prize. You don't have to imagine if you make a list of priorities and apply your uninhibited value toward them.

The "D" Word

I'm going to let you in on a little-known secret that will enable you to prioritize efficiently and effectively. But first, I must give a disclaimer.

This word is a taboo word that carries a negative connotation. The truth is that when applied in a negative and destructive way, I would never advocate for anyone applying this approach.

As an Aspirant, your vision is to be better and live better. Therefore, your aims are noble and well-intended. This isn't possible if you harbor any ill will toward others.

That said, in order to prioritize you must discriminate. More specifically, you must discriminate in favor of those things that are most important to you and against those thoughts, emotions, words and deeds that do not align with your vision.

Frankly, this isn't a novel concept. Most people, businesses, teams, governments, groups, clubs and organizations discriminate as a matter of principle. At least the successful ones do. When you remove the hateful, oppressive, and malicious application of the word, then what you're left with is a person or collective body that knows what matters and shows it by investing all of its value toward it.

Let me be clear—discrimination that is unjust or prejudicial that treats people as inferior and denies a person his or her basic human rights is not the type of discrimination I'm promoting. That goes against the fundamental narrative of The Poise Game, which suggests that if each person deliberately follows the path to his or her vision, then compassion for one another will be the result.

In this instance, I'm giving you the freedom to discriminate in the positive sense of the word. I believe when you are honest about your aims and feel empowered to invest all that you have toward it, then we all benefit.

Compromise and its Drawbacks

I've put a lot of emphasis on the importance of prioritizing what's important to you. You may be wondering: if I'm not prioritizing, then what am I doing?

The answer is—you are compromising.

So many people espouse that you can never get everything you desire. There's a general sense that at some point you should be prepared to compromise your desires, positions, interests, and other things because compromise is just a part of life.

Apparently, of the things that are guaranteed in life, there's death, taxes, and compromise.

Or maybe not.

What if you didn't have to compromise?

What if you could always make deliberate decisions that aligned with your vision for yourself and your life?

Well you don't have to compromise and you can always make those decisions.

How?

You already know the answer—prioritize.

I have an aversion to the idea that you should ever willingly compromise anything you value.

If you do that, doesn't it mean that you value something else more?

And if not, doesn't it mean you're conflicted if you're willingly choosing to apply your value toward things that don't align with your personal aims?

I'm not judging you if you still prefer to hold on to the notion that you should and must compromise, but let me at least present my case to you for abandoning that social construct.

Let's start with a definition of the word.

To compromise means to weaken the integrity and functionality of your vision through the use of unproductive thoughts, emotions, words, and deeds that are contrary to your highest ideals about yourself and your life.

If you compromise the structure of a bridge, then the risk for danger increases.

If you compromise the rechargeable battery of a cordless drill, then its performance will not provide the intended results.

If you compromise your position on a battlefield, then your mission will likely fail and your troops may be captured, or worse, killed.

You may think these are extreme examples, and I've failed to mention the compromise needed for relationships to survive.

Well let's consider those, too.

If you and your significant other compromise your interests, to "meet in the middle," then neither of you obtain what you desire, and will, in your own way, harbor some latent resentment that will present itself at another time and, if not resolved appropriately, in an unproductive way.

Adjusted Priorities are not Compromises

For clarity, this is not to say that you can't adjust your efforts based upon another's input or feedback.

In no way am I inferring that you can't adjust your priorities or how you think, emote, speak and act just because an idea comes from someone else.

Of course, you can.

On the contrary, I'm saying that any and all informed decisions are not compromises if they align with your vision.

That's not the same as compromising.

Here's how you can tell the difference.

If you choose to do something that wasn't an original thought of yours or is something that you're assuming would please another person and it aligns with your priorities or your broader vision, then this is not a compromise.

In this case, you've made an informed decision to choose differently for the benefit of your vision.

This is a wise choice and I strongly recommend it.

On the other hand, if you choose to do something that wasn't an original thought of yours or is something that you're assuming would please another person, and it doesn't align with your priorities or your broader vision, then this is a compromise.

In this case, you've made an ill-advised decision to choose something that conflicts with your vision.

This is an unwise choice and I strongly recommend against it.

Spend some time thinking about the decisions you've made that you would characterize as compromises.

How did you feel afterward?

I'm not talking about the immediate sense of altruism, that you sacrificed something for the greater good.

You know that feeling is not enduring.

I'm talking about the feeling of something, an

interest, a goal, perhaps a lifelong dream, left undone, and the energy you'd allocated for it not having an outlet, so it sits like a puddle of stagnant water inside you, and eventually becomes a cesspool that poisons your countenance.

You won't likely draw the connection to the moments of compromise because you've convinced yourself that they were for the greater good, but truthfully that's a delusion.

You know you're a derivative version of yourself and the life you're living pales in comparison to what, in your heart, it's supposed to be.

Once again, the decisions you choose that are contrary to your vision are compromises.

Never compromise.

Don't continue to mislabel the decisions that you make in consideration of others' perspectives and interests, and they align with your vision as compromises.

How can they be called compromises if they are productive?

If you were to improve the structural integrity of a bridge, would you define it as a compromise?

No, because it doesn't make sense.

Since we agree on that point, let's agree that you

will never again mislabel anything you choose to do that is productive as a compromise.

Prioritization is Difficult

Please don't be mistaken about the implementation of the method of prioritization.

You will probably still encounter situations that challenge you. You will face decisions that cause you to choose between your priorities and something or someone you love. And even when you know for certain your choice was the right one to make, you will feel the pain associated with grieving the separation, the loss, and the transition.

During this time, it's important that you recognize your grief doesn't mean you should question your decision or your loyalties or your respect or even your love.

You should only ask yourself this question: was this choice consistent with my priorities?

If your answer is yes, then it's okay for you to be sad for the potential hurt a loved one may experience because he or she doesn't completely understand. Likewise, it's okay for you to be sad because your choice led to the loss of or a significant change in the conditions of your relationship.

But you can also be content with the understanding

and knowledge that your choice was not taken lightly and was informed by your priorities that lead to productive thoughts, emotions, words, and deeds. You are content to do whatever is possible to make your vision a reality because in that reality, you are the best version of yourself and you are living your best life.

Priorities Can Change

By the way, did I mention your priorities can change?

Don't be upset with me because the reason they can change is because you can change.

Think about change as another word for evolve or mature. In that context, change doesn't mean problems. It means possibilities. Each time you experience or learn something new, change occurs. That's why change must be a welcome part of your journey.

Remember change means growth, maturity, experience, and progress. You should embody evolution in the sense that you are always learning, you are always applying what you're learning and, when you understand the reciprocal benefit, you are also always sharing what you've learned and applied. This should be happening from the cellular level to what's perceivable by the human eye.

So, when you sense that your priorities need to change, then you should follow these steps.

1. Review your vision.

When you review your vision, that means you're looking at the images you've included on your vision board. You should reflect upon the reason you selected those particular images and consider whether or not they best convey the specific ideals they represent. If they don't, then update them with ones that do. If they do, then soak in the imagery and visualize it as it will be when you attain it.

2. Assess your priorities for relevance.

When you assess your priorities, this means you are looking at your priorities list. You should first check to see if your priorities align with your vision. If there are any conflicts, then determine if the priority should be represented on the vision board and if you believe it should be, then update your vision board accordingly. If you believe the priority shouldn't be reflected, then remove it. If you have no conflicts, then be grateful for knowing what's important to you.

3. Reduce the rank or remove priorities that are less important.

If you identify items on your priority list that have dropped in terms of importance or you believe they no longer should belong on your list, then lower the position or remove them accordingly.

4. Increase the rank or add priorities that are more important.

If you identify items on your priority list that have raised in terms of importance or items not yet on your list that you believe should belong on your list, then raise the position or add them accordingly.

5. Implement and validate your list by completing an E2A relating to your number one priority.

In excellent Aspirant fashion, it's important that you affirm what you believe is important by immediately choosing to complete an E2A. This puts a cap on the changed priority list. It gives you a win to connect to your effort, reminding you that change is okay, and in this case it's appropriate because it sets conditions for you to continue progressing toward your vision.

Do not become wedded to your priorities for their own sake. If they no longer align with your vision or they drop in terms of importance, you shouldn't feel any shame about changing them. In that case, be humble and prioritize progress over pride.

Compromise Traps

Sometimes you don't intend to compromise, but you still find yourself easily drawn in by its lures. Here are a few things for which you should exercise caution—not because they're bad, but because they're the bait used in the compromise trap.

First, exercise caution toward anything that has familiarity.

There is no easier way to get you to forget your priorities than to roll out the red carpet of nostalgia. This seemingly harmless tactic will have you longing for the good old days, when you should be focused.

Second, exercise caution toward all non-expedient activities.

Take a moment to account for each thought, emotion, word, and deed you have. Consider the activities that led to their creation. Now count how many of them are expedient in terms of what's important to you.

If most of them meet the threshold, then

congratulations. You're probably in the clear. If half of them or more fall below the cutline, then that's okay. Don't judge or beat yourself up. You can address them by acknowledging the choices that you made that resulted in this observation and reducing that number down to an amount that you choose.

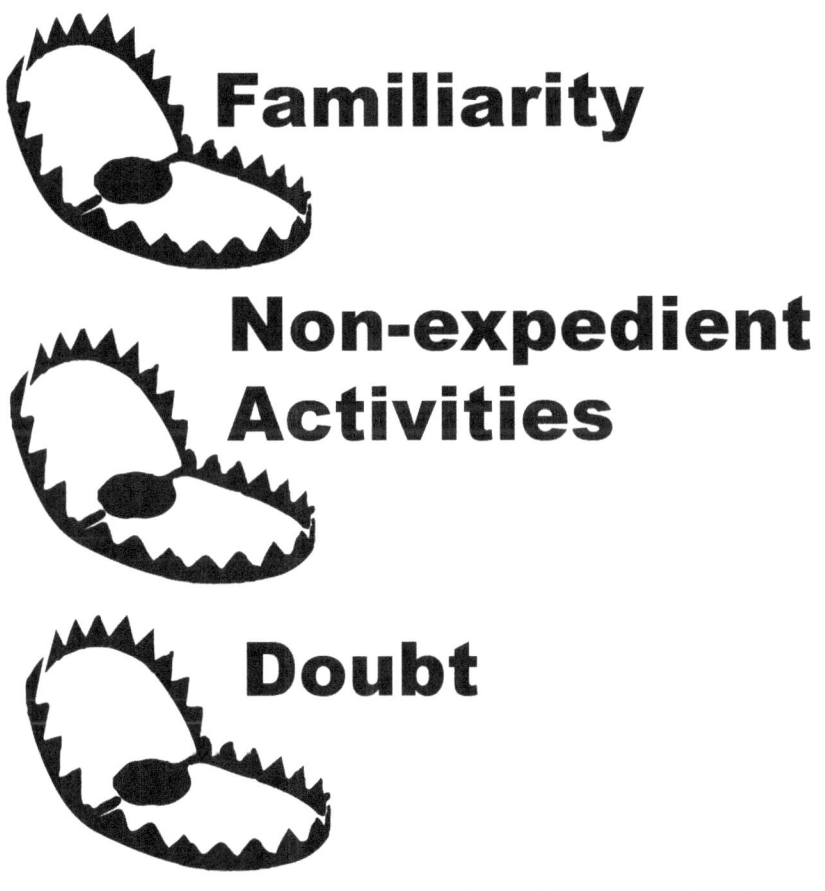

Compromise Traps

In fact, replace the non-expedient activities with some productive ones. By now, as an Aspirant, you should have in mind a few go-to generic E2As you can do to pass the time. Go ahead and complete them. This is not to say you can't do anything that isn't expedient as some non-expedient activities morph into E2As because of their utility. It may be that they are the one thing in that moment that help you maintain your sanity or bring you joy and satisfaction.

Third, exercise caution toward doubt.

A lack in faith can only come from an uncertainty about your vision and your priorities. Spend the time ensuring your vision is the choice you desire. Verify that your priorities align with your vision. Once those two are addressed, then you can be confident in your choices because they are productive. The more productive choices you make, the more your faith will increase. This is because you will have evidence that your faith isn't arbitrary or futile. It's specific and fruitful.

These are all traps and tricks that can subtly keep you from achieving your vision.

The ability to know what's important to you and apply the value of your energy, time, space, and resources toward it is a sign that you are an Aspirant who is committed to your vision. As you consider your priorities, there is one more method that is key for you to progress on your path.

I must warn you. This method may challenge everything you think you know and understand about the reasons you are making a conscious effort to make deliberate choices.

Your Intentions

"Always perform your duty efficiently and without attachment to the results, because by doing work without attachment one attains the Supreme."

Bhagavad Gita

Ask yourself this: if you did everything that you should to make progress toward your vision, would your good intentions be enough if you didn't get the outcomes you desire?

That's a reasonable question and one that you will wrestle with and, hopefully, discover your answer in this chapter. This is the final method you will learn to implement while playing The Poise Game.

All the other methods aimed to ensure you knew how to accept, wield and maintain your power. This method is different though because it teaches you that in order for you to truly become your best self and live your best life, you must abandon something you may believe is a necessary accompaniment to your journey.

Everything that you've been shown thus far in the game suggests that if you align your thoughts, emotions, words and deeds with your vision, then it will come to pass.

But what if it doesn't?

What if you have a clear vision of everything you could ever hope for and more, and you set out to do all the things you choose to do because, as far as you know, they are the relevant productive activities for your ideals, and you never arrive?

Is that okay?

Will you feel like you made all of those decisions—those choices—for nothing?

Are Good Intentions Enough?

As an Aspirant, your true success is when you recognize that the entirety of your beingness is the sum of your choices given the environmental factors in which they're made.

Having absolute faith that your vision is your created purpose—your duty—think, emote, speak and act with wholehearted, willful and well-meaning intentions, despite the subsequent outcomes.

The skill you seek to develop here is to be able to

act with good intentions without any expectations.

You must lay aside all of your expectations and commit yourself to the purpose that drives your efforts.

In the fortress of your resolute mind, the knowledge of your vision equals a truth untarnished and uninhibited by momentary happenings. You are content with performing your E2As because they are your choice and you choose that which is designed to accomplish your vision whether you reach it or not.

What Makes Your Intentions Good?

What makes your intentions good is that they are congruent with your path and they do not seek to disrupt the path of anyone else. You can probably think of several reasons that would make this a challenging standard to uphold.

What if you aim to improve the lives of people struggling with drug addiction? Won't your aims conflict with those of the drug peddler who sells drugs?

I see your questions and answer them with one of my own.

Why do you assume that the drug dealer's vision matches with what he or she is currently doing?

Perhaps this is what the drug dealer believes is the only and best option available. When a person seeks to benefit from the destruction of another, then I don't believe that represents that person's best self living his or her best life.

Be aware that on the dark side of your good intentions is a persona of moral superiority which causes you to become the judge, jury and, as history has shown in far too many cases, the executioner, who condemns others as irredeemable without fully understanding that what you observe is just a snapshot of them along their journey.

There is no conflict with another person's vision when your aim is to help and not control, coerce, judge or condemn.

Good intentions are your deliberate and self-regulated thoughts, emotions, words and deeds that seek productivity, joy and love.

Expectations may seem harmless. I mean, who doesn't have them? Isn't it reasonable for you to tie your good intentions to your expected outcomes?

The Problem with Expectations

It's only reasonable because it's a common practice; however, here's a better question you should ask yourself: Is it productive to tie my good intentions to my expected outcomes?

When you consider whether the behavior is productive, then you see that perhaps, though it is common, it isn't prudent.

Expectations have the uncanny ability to ruin your experiences because whether it's good, successful or worthwhile is dependent upon something beyond your direct control.

When your expectations fail to occur, then you're left with the symptoms of emotions related to the feelings of loss, such as disappointment, anger, bitterness, shame and sickness.

Do I need to keep going?

And I don't have to prove this to you with stories and illustrations. You know this is true because you've personally experienced it.

Don't let a wordsmith tell you that this is all semantics and expectations really demonstrate your hope and faith. I can see how someone would come to that conclusion, but let me explain why it's a mischaracterization.

Hope and faith are both based upon your certainty of the possibility that a certain outcome can occur. It's you knowing that anything, even the impossible, is possible, but not guaranteed in the way you may think.

Expectation is based upon your sense of entitlement that you deserve to receive or experience a certain outcome because your actions warrant it. It's you demanding that this one thing or these particular things better happen.

There is no requirement for you to expect anything from your actions.

You know that, right? A

nd because of that I give you the freedom to throw your expectations away.

Life Without Expectations

There is a chance someone with the proverbial axe to grind will scrutinize my life, my words and my behaviors to determine if I'm practicing what I'm preaching.

Guess what?

I welcome it.

And what you will find, if you decide to look deeply, is that there are times when I do have the symptoms of unfulfilled expectations—feelings of loss, disappointment, anger, bitterness, shame, sickness—which means that, at least in those moments, I had expectations

I am certain that it is best for you, me and

everyone to abandon expectations, but I'm not advocating that you are wrong if you have them. The presence of expectations or its symptoms in you and your life should not lead to an indictment. You won't be charged with failing to live up to the Aspirant policies, regulations, code of ethics and statutes. You should not feel any shame when these emotions arise.

If you observe expectations or its symptoms in yourself or if someone, especially a member of your TAN, indicates that these things seem to be present, then that's okay.

It's important that when you have the time, perhaps in a moment of meditation or prayer or while on a walk or during your commute to work, you acknowledge the emotions you feel. When you experience them, it is an indicator that you have an unfulfilled expectation or you have an expectation that you sense will go unmet.

This simply means you are feeling or beginning to feel a sense of loss. That's what it is. Something perceptually was taken from you — something you care about and something that matters— and you must grieve the loss.

Allow yourself to grieve productively by

considering the E2As, GAInS adventures and Vision Board imagery that are associated with the expectation. Be grateful that nothing can take them away because they did happen. They represent a win and the process of winning through your deliberate choices based upon what you can control, and that thing you can control is singular—yourself.

Though the feeling of loss is real and must be grieved to resolve it, the feeling of gratitude is equally real. The special thing about gratitude is that it's designed to be enduring through the range of emotions because it's one of the emotions that can universally exist concurrently with every other emotion. The foundation of your gratitude is found in the truth, which you have the ability to choose and use to shape your present existence through poise.

Refrain from having expectations, but there is no punishment if you do. When it occurs, explore the symptoms to uncover the points of gratitude that exist. They're there if you look closely.

To experience sadness, anger, bitterness, depression, disappointment, shame or sickness at the same time you experience gratitude doesn't mean you're conflicted. It means you're complex.

As you go through a period of loss, it will have an indefinite life span. No one can tell you how long is the appropriate duration. During your grieving period you experience the rollercoaster effect of peaks and valleys, especially regarding your thoughts and emotions.

When you observe, you're experiencing gratitude in the midst of your grief, and this indicates you're at a peak, so I want to encourage you to determine if this is the peak where you choose to transition from your grieving period.

If you sense it's time to resolve your grief and transition, then I recommend you make a deliberate choice to do so. You don't need to announce it to people, but oftentimes it's good to formalize transitions with something to represent the milestone. I think choosing a custom or generic E2A for you to complete is a good way to do this.

On the other hand, if you sense that more grieving is necessary, then allow yourself the freedom to do so without shame or judgment. Just monitor your peaks and valleys to ensure that you're not plunging deep into a never-ending abyss.

Your TAN is key for you to stay accountable to your vision and it helps mitigate against the impact of expectations or the loss you sense when they go unfulfilled so your journey isn't derailed.

Remember that your peaks are the opportunities for you to choose to exit your grieving period. By the way, in case you were wondering if this approach to grief could work in other areas, the answer is yes it does. This applies to grief associated with unmet expectations as well as grief associated with other losses.

Two Expectations–Farmer or Fisherman

My perspective about expectations may seem extreme, so let me temper it a bit. I admit that there are some expectations that have utility and should remain connected with the good intentions and subsequent actions that generate them.

Am I back-peddling?

I don't think so. But let me describe why two approaches to expectations can exist in the same dimensional plane.

The expectations that I believe are okay to possess are those that deal with your intentions, also projected via your conveyance faculties, but are minimally impacted, supported and processed through a filter prior to the result. In fact, these expectations are possible because you directly take them from ideation to fruition. Since you have actions associated with each step, you are observing the outcome in the making, and therefore it's reasonable for you to have expectations.

The expectations I described earlier in the chapter are those that deal with your intentions that are projected via your conveyance faculties, and are impacted, supported and otherwise processed through a filter that ultimately arrives at a result that is not entirely of your making, but one that is inspired by your thoughts, emotions, words and deeds. In this occasion, you should lay aside your expectations and entirely resolve yourself to be content with your good intentions.

So when considering whether your expectations are productive, you should run them through what I call "The Farmer or the Fisherman Test."

You see, the farmer represents the situation when you should have expectations because you control each functional step leading to your desired outcome. If your vision is to be a farmer, then you can be, do and have what is required and expect to eventually pick your bounty from the field. You can prepare the ground and plant the seed. Ensure the seed receives water, sunlight and other nutrients

FARMER
Your direct actions are determining factors for the indended outcome.

Expectations 👍

FISHERMAN
Your direct actions are contributing factors for the indended outcome.

Expectations 👎

The Famer and The Fisherman Test

from within the soil. You can take deliberate steps to keep pests and other vermin from destroying or taking the seedlings prematurely. You can allow the appropriate time to elapse and return to your lot to pick the desired and expected outcome, which is your harvest.

Now the fisherman represents the situation when you should abstain from any expectations because there are several externalities that impact whether you attain the desired outcome. If your vision is to be a fisherman, then you can be, do and have what is required and still not go home with any fish. You can have the requisite knowledge and experience. You can accurately apply it. You understand the waters, the equipment, the breeds and the bait, and still not make the catch because the result is dependent upon the collective effort, not just your own.

"The Farmer or the Fisherman Test" goes like this.

Ask yourself these two yes or no questions:

Are you involved in each step from concept to completion? If yes, then, like the farmer, it's safe to have expectations. Your focused efforts will more than likely result in your desired outcomes. It's like doing simple mathematical equations.

Are you mainly the idea person, but the end result relies upon several external factors, few if any are in the realm of your ability to control let alone influence? If yes, then, like the fisherman, don't burden yourself with expectations. Because that's exactly what they will become— a burden. If the outcome falls short, then for an undetermined duration of time into your future you will carry the heavy load.

Whichever one you answer yes to, then manage expectations as prescribed.

Your value — energy, time, space and resources — can be applied in any areas of your choosing that align with your vision or you can choose to invest toward mourning unrealized expectations.

Just like with everything else, the purpose here is to develop your poise, to give you a discipline of deliberate self-control. You play the game to win. You win each time you make a choice and are content with it because you know you are writing the script for your life, and in it, when you're applying all The Poise Game tools and methods, you are your own champion.

Your Beginning

"If there is a secret for greater self-control, the science points to one thing: the power of paying attention. It's training the mind to recognize when you're making a choice, rather than running on autopilot."

Kelly McGonigal

In every situation you find yourself, from the easy and insignificant to the complex and momentous, you have a choice.

The Poise Game is designed to help you systematize your approach to achieving your life's vision through the development of your self-control—your poise.

Over the course of the previous 11 chapters, you've learned everything you need to know to be an Aspirant who is empowered with the background, the tools and the methods to begin your journey toward becoming your best self and living your best life. If you take nothing else from what you've read in this book, I hope you will take hold of your autonomy.

You can choose to make decisions that contribute to your betterment and progress on the path toward your vision or you can choose to make decisions that are compromising to your integrity and to your well-being that lead to discontentment and an unfulfilling life.

Is there anything else that you need to read to be convinced?

If so, then you fall into a very popular club. You're among the majority of people who want someone to show them all the answers without them having to do any work to obtain the benefit. This is not a judgment. It's just an observation from my personal experience.

There is no side-stepping around this fact: You will not reach your goal, you will not attain your prize, you will not become your best self or live your best life without choices that require your deliberate, focused and consistent effort.

Conditioning for the Aspirant Experience

Your experience as an Aspirant will be like that of a body that aims to be more fit. It must endure the strain related to the quantity of repetitions and the resistance of the weights during exercise in order to increase in size, strength and endurance. The demands placed on it will cause the muscles to fatigue and breakdown. They will require proper nutrition, rest and recovery. But with intention, attention and unrelenting effort, the body is on the path to fitness, which is the desired outcome.

This book has outlined several steps in terms of creating and using tools and applying methodological approaches. If you are serious about making steady and productive progress, then you will complete the tasks presented throughout the book.

If it all seems like too much to do, then just spend some time creating a list of generic E2As and build your Poise Deck. At a minimum, you can begin by choosing to complete simple tasks that slowly but surely contribute to larger objectives.

In order to truly begin your Aspirant journey, you must have the following three tools created as a minimum: Vision board, GAInS and Poise Deck. Without these items, you're more like an Aspirant-candidate—a person who sees the value the tools and methods will bring to his or her life, but who is unwilling to commit the value investment that is part of the start-up costs to really play the game.

A Fool-proof, Self-investment

If you're wavering about whether this is worth it, let me explain something to you. Every bit of your value—your energy, time, space and resources—that you apply toward creating your Poise Game tools and learning the methods is an investment into yourself.

There are few investments in life that you can make that have zero risk and 100 percent reward.

This is one of them.

Let's say you don't buy into the system or something about the prescribed methodologies doesn't jive with your preferences. In the end, you will still benefit because everything was done with your interests in mind.

All of the choices I recommend for and against are based upon what you have determined is your best self and best life.

You've consulted with you and you've made decisions about you for you.

There should be no wasted effort. All of your value stays within the economy of you.

The worst case is that you try The Poise Game tools and methods and just don't like it for you, but you still like the idea of the power of your choice so you continue your journey empowered to do what the game is designed to systematically develop in the first place—your poise.

Also, remember that throughout the book you may have noticed I'm making recommendations, but the implied message is that the decision is yours to make.

It's your choice.

If you want to modify everything about the Poise Game to suit your preferences, then have at it.

If you prefer to only implement one or two things and never apply any of the others, then I applaud the fact that you have chosen what you believe is best for what you need.

On the other extreme, if you want to follow everything as prescribed all the way to playing your GAInS with the d-8, using your Poise Deck liberally, tracking your Poise Points on your Poise Aspirant Dashboard, then I'm grateful that you recognize the value of the tools and methods and see their utility in your journey.

Either way, these are all your choices.

Part of the reason they are provided is that I want to assist you on your journey; but more importantly I want to let you know that you are already demonstrating your ability to make deliberate choices by reading this book and determining which tools and methods to create and apply. In these efforts, you are demonstrating poise.

But as I stated, I recommend that as soon as possible you take the time to create at least the three Poise tools described above.

Don't wait.

First is your vision board.

If you're a busy person, schedule an appointment with yourself and be prepared to schedule a few, if necessary, so you can get this critical component of your success complete. Identify the aspects of your ideal self and ideal life that you desire and find imagery, photos and words that depict them to display. Take your thoughts and transfer them to a physical, or if you prefer, a digital medium. Write out your Personal Mission Statement and your Personal Conviction Mantra and commit yourself to reciting them as often as you can.

In the business world, there is a concept called an elevator pitch. The idea is that if you were stuck in an elevator riding with a person and only had that moment to sell him or her on your idea, then you would focus your presentation on the most significant aspects. It's generally about one to two minutes. Your Vision Board with PMS and PCM are your elevator pitch about you to yourself and those with whom you desire to share it.

The work involved in this step and described in chapters four and five is critically important if progressing toward your vision is truly your aim. You must take the time to complete this transfer from the conceptual to the concrete because there will inevitably be times when you experience mental blocks that impede or impair your access to your internal vision. The ability to stay focused and remain steadfast during these times will be based upon several factors, including the people and resources you have available to support you. This is something that is within your control.

When you make the prudent choice to complete your vision board, you will have put yourself in a position of advantage. Whenever you experience uncertainty or are faced with multiple options that appear to be good, then you can evaluate them against what you've envisioned. If nothing seems to fit, then now you don't have to waste your value by even considering it any further. Choose to let it go and leave it to whomever is the right person to invest his or her value toward it. If only some of it matches with your vision, then put aside the parts that don't and consider when you would be interested in achieving the parts that do. If you have clarity on how to do it and when to do it, then perhaps you can add it to your GAInS as an adventure. If it's not apparent, then ensure it's reflected on your vision board and table the more detailed efforts for later. This is the utility of the Vision Board and why it's vital that you put in the work to create it.

The second item that requires some thoughtful consideration is your annual GAInS.

Identifying and selecting GAInS adventures to accomplish each year can be time consuming and it can be challenging, especially if you aren't sure how to do certain things or you aren't even sure how to develop a plan of action.

If you discover that just getting started seems like an insurmountable task, then that's okay. Give yourself the freedom and flexibility to be a novice at things. I haven't explicitly stated this yet, but I will right now for your benefit. There will be, and, in my belief, should be images on your vision board and adventures on your GAInS, E2As, T2D and Poise Deck for which you are a novice of the highest order. The point is that there will be things that you choose to do that make you feel uncomfortable, incapable and out of your league.

You will have several experiences in which the only way you can accurately characterize your performance is: I suck. That's okay. And perhaps it's true for the moment. Self-deprecating humor can become a great technique for you as you get beyond your pride that would otherwise block you from achieving your highest ideals as long as it can avoid a few moments of embarrassment. If you don't know how to begin with making one of your vision images a reality, then here's a simple approach.

Research a person who has done or is currently doing the thing represented in the image. Consider the steps he or she took leading to achieving that milestone. Take the time to do the research. Then consider making those notable items your GAInS Adventures. Sometimes it only takes one adventure to achieve an image. Sometimes it takes several.

Either way, there is a universal truth that you must know. It comes from an ancient Hebrew proverb: "What has been is what will be, and what has been done is what will be done; there is nothing new under the sun." For you this means, if you envision it, that it is not only possible, but if you look deep within yourself and as far out into the corners of the universe, you will find the way to achieve your aims. And even if you don't find the way, there will be so many joyful experiences along a purposeful path to finding something you wholeheartedly desire, that it will be worth the value of your lifetime.

Finally, the third Poise Game tool I recommend you make in earnest is your Poise Deck.

There is something fun about listing things that you would love to do if you weren't so busy and obligated by the social constructs of life. Once your deck is complete, then you can begin to fill small gaps of idle time with your E2As. Soon you'll discover yourself thinking about how you could just do certain E2As at specific times without even shuffling the deck and drawing the cards. The deck is truly a token, but with function. However, the ultimate goal is that you have your Poise Deck E2As memorized and you've had enough experiences that you know which E2A is best suited and most expedient in certain times and places that you choose to do them without even employing the physical deck.

Obviously, I believe that all the tools bring value to your experience playing the Poise Game, but this isn't about what I believe. It's about what aligns with your vision. If you're unsure, then I recommend you go through the effort of building each tool as described in the chapters. The work done there will allow you to dig deep to give yourself the freedom to imagine what's possible. Maybe there are dreams that were put aside because you began to feel they were no longer possible. Now you can explore them. You can revise them. You can believe in them, again. You are worth the value of your investment into yourself.

The Four Methods Can Provide Instantaneously Results

Apply Four Methods for Immediate Results

Now let's talk about the methods.

The methods can be applied immediately and irrespective of which tools you decide to use.

If you're at least telling yourself that you're sure things will work out, then that's a good place to start.

The four methods presented in this book—let's abbreviate them to be (1) Choice, (2) Mindset, (3) Priorities, and (4) Intentions— are key to helping you to develop the ability to demonstrate self-control in your situations.

I've found that these four methods, when applied,

can immediately begin to change the perception of your circumstances. When your perception changes, then it enlightens you to other opportunities that you couldn't perceive before because your former perspective made you blind to them.

Regarding choice, you must recognize that, even though there are a lot of things that are beyond your control, whatever is happening within your realm of influence is up to you. For this reason, you are not a victim of circumstance. You're a victor of choice. What's tricky is that if you decide to be a victim, that's still a choice, except in this case you're relinquishing your power to an external entity. If you're going to make any choice, then choose to be your own champion.

Regarding mindset, there is a three-part way of looking at your mindset. The first is be, which is about who you are. Second is do, which represents your activities. And third is have, which is the resources that manifest. If you are the image of what you aspire to be, then you are doing the right things and if you're doing the right things then you have the right things. The Be-Do-Have triad helps you to then consider your conveyance faculties, which include your thoughts, emotions, words and deeds.

Choice
Mindset
Priorities
Intensions

The Four Methods

If what you are conveying is ever incongruent with who you choose to be, what you choose to do and what you choose to have, then you can and should make a deliberate choice to change it.

Regarding priorities, you get to choose what's important in your life. And with that you have the freedom and autonomy to apply the value of your energy, time, space and resources toward the things you deem important. Whenever there is a question of what efforts get your value, the answer is simple because by having explicit priorities, you know that they represent the most prudent and productive aspects for your life. In the long run, your efforts and value investments toward your priorities will be extremely rewarding because they align with your vision.

Regarding intentions, you are willing to think, emote, speak and act in accordance with your highest ideals about yourself and your life despite the time it takes to receive the desirable outcomes and even if the desired outcomes never occur. Your intentions must be supreme. You must be content in your conveyance faculties and your confidence rests in the knowledge that your intentions are aimed at progressing you toward your vision so that makes them good. You have faith that your well-intended efforts will result in the outcomes you seek, but even if they don't, you remain content in what you have the power to influence — your self-control.

If your intentions mean well regarding yourself and others, if they seek to edify, construct, add value, demonstrate compassion and love and are overall things that would receive a good report, then no matter what happens as a result of them, you can be content. This is why you would choose to have good intentions without expectations. By detaching your intentions from their desired outcomes, you remove the possibility of experiencing the negative emotions related to loss, such as anger, shame and disappointment. This will be because you realize you haven't wasted your value. In fact, you can be grateful for the experiences along the journey of your life because you are fulfilled.

You are Ready to Climb

Friend, as an Aspirant, you have arrived at this point and are primed with the tools and methods to start your journey to taking control of your experiences and to deliberately become the person and establish the life of which you would be proud.

You're at the bottom of the mountain and your vision is at its peak.

You have a choice. You can turn away because you're unwilling to do the work that it takes to get you to the destination. You can continue to stay in the same place making excuses about why you're not progressing. Or you can start climbing, inch by inch, toward hope, purpose and fulfilment.

Others, like you, have made the climb by having

a vision of success, the courage to start, the perseverance to keep going, and the gratitude for every day you get another opportunity to climb.

You are an Aspirant.

All that remains is your decision: choose today to start the climb. You are worth the investment of your energy, time, space and resources. Look within yourself and see the vivid imagery of your highest ideals. Give yourself the freedom to employ every effort—every thought, emotion, word and deed—toward doing the work that leads to your purpose.

You can start climbing now.

I'll see you at the top.

Your Afterlife

"Do for this life as if you live forever, do for the afterlife as if you die tomorrow."

Ali ibn Abi Talib

You should be proud of yourself.

You have every reason to be if you've arrived at this point.

Up until now, you've focused on the perspective, methods and tools that lead you to becoming your best self and living your best life. What could be more ideal than that?

Well, let me tell you. If you went through the effort of molding yourself and manufacturing your life into what you envisioned, then you probably would want to know if there was something more. You'd want to know if there was something that's related to your efforts so you know they weren't wasted, but something that transcends what you may have presumed was the apex of your possibilities.

Now, I want to be clear—if you are currently implementing everything prescribed in chapters one through 12, then I wholeheartedly believe that you will experience a relatively good life based upon most descriptions and standards. The reason I say your life will be relatively good is because I also know that there will be something missing if you only focus on this life and disregard the life after.

Yes. I believe there is an afterlife, and your choices in this one will determine how you spend it. If you applied the principles in this book, there is no doubt you will be rewarded with temporal contentment; but I believe if you choose to do everything you do for the God of the Holy Bible and not for men, then He will reward you with gifts that are eternal.

The greatest gift, which is the endowment of a glorified body and an experience of eternal life in the presence of God, comes by confessing that His son, Jesus Christ, lived a perfect life, was crucified and then resurrected from the dead and now is seated next to God in the heavens.

Spiritual Virtues

In chapter one I shared with you a Bible passage that led me to create The Poise Game. The background to that passage is that it describes not just any kind of virtues, but spiritual virtues. Virtues that represent the epitome of goodness in this world and the world after.

When you look at the virtues, they all appear to be nouns of which you must possess. You must have love, joy, peace, patience, kindness, goodness, faithfulness, gentleness and self-control. But I believe the idea of them of objects misses the mark. If you think these are virtues that you must have, then it's possible for you to absolve yourself of their associated responsibilities when they appear to be elusive and just beyond your grasp.

However, one virtue, self-control, which I've re-branded as poise, had a different quality that made it more difficult to project the responsibility for its absence on the environment or on another person. I mean, it is self-control, which, in the adapted words of comedian Katt Williams, means control of your mutha' lovin' self. He was actually speaking about self-esteem, but you get my drift. The point is you are responsible for controlling yourself.

As I began to consider this responsibility in light of the other virtues, I discovered something—by demonstrating self-control or poise, as I call it, you could develop it into a habit as well as all of the other virtues.

So why would you do this?

Well because a virtuous life is you becoming your ideal self and living your ideal life.

The Poise Game also made me realize something else. The other virtues, just like self-control, aren't things you have; they're things you do. We just need to call them by their active name.

Of the group, love is probably the simplest because in order to have love, you love. Then we

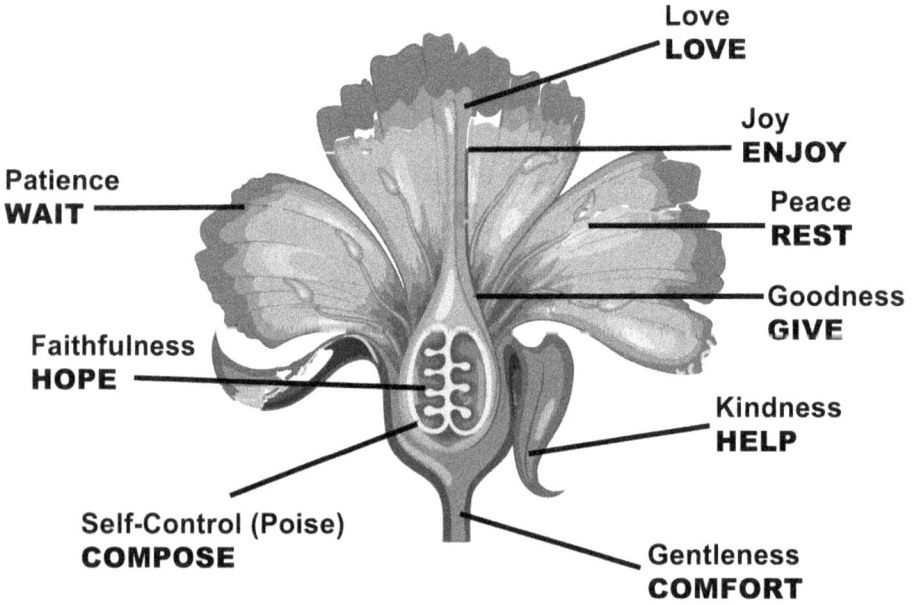

Spiritual (Eternal) Virtues

can apply the same approach to the rest. You must enjoy to have joy. You must rest to have peace. You must wait to have patience. You must help to have kindness. You must give to have goodness. You must hope to have faith. You must comfort to have gentleness. And you must compose to have poise. From this evolved perspective, you can see that from the beginning you had the option to choose all of the virtues.

The spiritual virtues are like the parts of a flower. Each part is special and they all work in harmony to contribute the vital aspects that make the flower what it is designed to be.

Poise to Choose the Savior

Poise as a virtue is not the most important, but the value of its utility is that it helps you recognize that everything you are and everything you experience is your choice.

Like a music director at the lectern in front of his orchestra, you are composing yourself and your life. And you can make the choice about your afterlife. You can choose to accept Jesus the Messiah of the Christian faith as your Savior.

What exactly is He saving you from?

And, if you can have a relatively good life without making this choice, then why would you?

That's a great question.

Here's your answer.

Jesus saves you from an afterlife that would be worse than the present one you're currently making every effort to escape.

You would choose Him even with the prospects of a relatively good life because if you're the type of person who would go to this degree to experience what you've perceived as ideal, then the moment you realized that there is more to the story, you are compelled to make the choice that leads to that subsequent destination.

There is a fitting verse from the Holy Bible that describes the futility of stopping your efforts short of choosing Christ: "What good would it do to get everything you want and lose you, the real you?"

Do me a favor.

Strongly consider what I shared above.

What do I get out of it? Frankly, the value for me is intrinsic. I get the joy of knowing that one more person took the faithful step toward eternal truth to experience his or her highest ideals in this life and the one to come.

But just like everything else in this book, it's not about what I get. It's really about what you get and what the people with whom you encounter receive as a result of your choice.

Your entire aim is to become your best self and live your best life. I'm recommending that you don't stop short with the present life and neglect the next one.

If you're willing to consider it, then let me give you some action steps to take.

With the first step, I have some reading for you to do. It'll be an hour of your time that is worth it in terms of setting the context for what I've suggested.

You need to read some selected passages from the Bible:

1. The book of Matthew, chapters five through seven

2. The entire book of Ecclesiastes.

I recommend you read from any of the following versions for clarity: New International Version, New Living Translation, Common English Version, Christian Standard Bible and The Message.

You can read any version if you'd like, but these are the ones I've found easiest for people to understand. Also, you can find them online via any web search application.

The reason I want you to read that portion of

Matthew is because it is Jesus speaking to an audience of people about principles for living a life of purpose. If I'm asking you to accept Him as your Savior, then I believe it's important you hear directly from Him.

Perhaps you hate everything you read. In that case, I appreciate your consideration. But I'm confident that's not how you'll feel afterward.

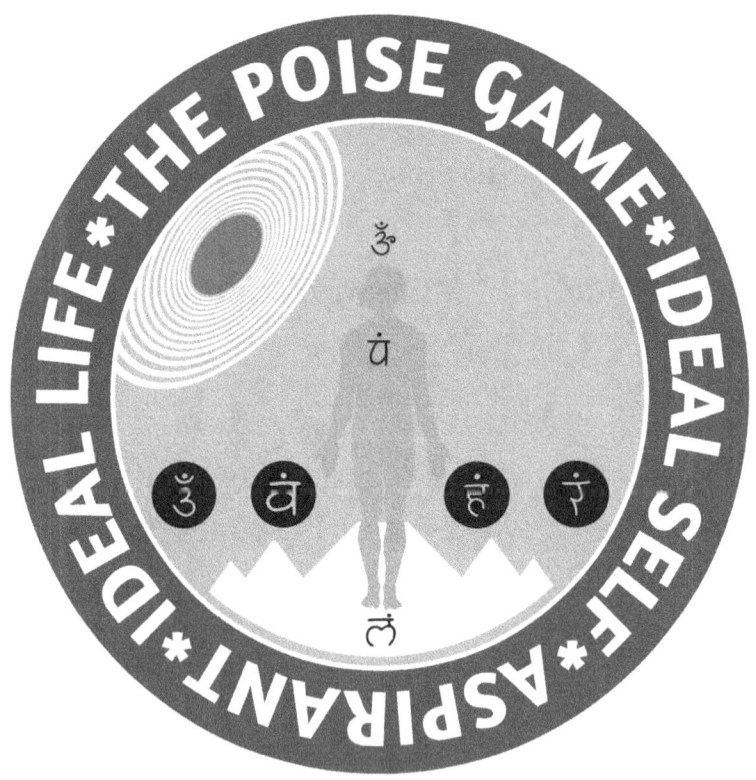

The Poise Aspirant Seal

The reason I want you to read the entire book of Ecclesiastes is because the authorship is attributed to Solomon, a Hebrew king who was acclaimed for his wisdom.

According to the Bible, God endowed Solomon with this wisdom making him the wisest man to ever live before his time and afterward. Ecclesiastes is Solomon writing at a point in his life where he was tired of making wise decisions.

Apparently, he'd made them all.

He'd earned more wealth than a person could spend in a thousand lifetimes. So he began intentionally making foolish choices.

During his foolishness, he admits that he denied himself nothing his heart desired. With the unlimited resources and access he had, you can only imagine what he did during this time.

It demonstrates that with the poise perspective, methods and tools you can become your ideal self and live the ideal life in this lifetime. He also presents a case for what is the most important thing you can choose when considering this life and the next one. There won't be any spoilers here. You must read Ecclesiastes if you choose to know what the wisest man to ever live recommends.

The second step is that you find a Christian

church or Christian person with whom you can speak to discuss what you are considering. I don't expect you to make such an important and life-changing decision simply from reading these texts. It's in the realm of the possible, but not expected, of course. I want you to ask him or her tough questions. If you don't get the answers, then ask that person to direct you to someone who can answer them.

The third step is to take a moment to apply the graduated poise pattern to this situation. Review the information you know and recall your experiences considering the newly-acquired knowledge. Assess the state of your life. If you're reading this book, then I think it's safe to assume you aren't yet your best self or living your best life. Where are you on your path and how does your assessment change considering what you've recently learned about this option regarding the afterlife? Refine your perspective considering the new information you read and the answers to your questions. Focus and identify your priorities. Take note if they've changed or if they're the same. Make a choice to live for Jesus Christ or to live for something else. Like everything in this book, this choice is yours to make. Obviously, I hope you choose to accept

Jesus as your Savior, but if that is not your choice, then I respect that, too. Either way, we've arrived at the destination you sought from the beginning.

You began this book with the hopes of discovering ways and acquiring the means to progress toward the ideal you and the ideal life. Along the way you've developed your own abilities and practiced making choices that steadily lead to your vision.

Continue to make progress. Stay encouraged. Share what you know and what you've learned in this book with others. Imagine a world full of people who are joyful and lack nothing because they are everything they could have imagined and their lives are everything they ever could've hoped.

"You are special because you are you.

You are capable, and you are equipped.

You just need to be willing and demonstrate it by each choice you make every moment of your life.

If you have poise, then you can be your best self and you can live your best life.

You can find infinite peace in your heart.

You can have that life now," said the voice.

Epilogue

With both hands and all the strength you can muster, you pull yourself to the top of the crest.

You take a knee, but not because of exhaustion. Amazingly you feel more energized than ever. You kneel in homage to what this moment signifies. You are standing upon the summit of the mountain of your highest ideals—your vision's peak.

You take a moment to scan the surroundings. You look over the ledge and realize how far you've come since you began the Aspirant's journey.

You consider all of the adventures that contributed to the success of your efforts. Each and every activity you chose to complete that moved you closer and closer to your desired outcomes. You are overcome with gratitude.

Then, you sense a familiar energy and turn to see the red glow slightly to the eastern edge of the summit.

This light served as a beacon, constantly calling you, guiding you, encouraging you and correcting you to arrive at this time and place. You move toward it slowly. You don't have any fear. Your steady approach is reverential.

As you near the red light and come within a few steps from it, you are immediately flushed with what you know as the eternal virtues, which are love, joy, peace, patience, kindness, goodness, gentleness, faithfulness and—self-control.

Now that you are directly beneath the red light, you look into it excited to know the source of its power.

Before your eyes, the light transforms and an image appears. It's an image you've seen before. It's an image you know intricately. In fact, it's not just an image, it's a reflection.

You see yourself now as you've seen yourself in your visions. In your reflection you see the evidence of your efforts to manifest your highest ideals about who you choose to be and the life you choose to live. You are standing here now being your best self living your best life.

You've reached your apogee.

Just as you realize the joy of the knowledge that the source of the beacon's power was in you and with you all along, the reflection disappears, wisping away into the clouds.

It doesn't take long before you see something— it's a vision.

Your vision evolves and your new purpose reveals itself.

It's you assisting other Aspirants to discover, make progress toward and achieve their visions for themselves.

You are no longer just an Aspirant.

Now you are also a Guide.

The Poise Game Tools

Here are examples of The Poise Game Tools based upon a fictional person named Sam.

Vision Board

First, use the Character translation techniques, comprising the Five As, the Five Sensory Descriptors and the Eight Adventure Categories to explain your ideal self.

Second, use the World translation techniques, comprising the Environmental Factors and the Five Sensory Descriptors to explain your ideal life.

Sam's Character: Vision Board Part I

Five A's
A1 Cool nerdy; 90's retro; Slim; broad shoulders
A2 Dry humor; quiet; serious; mysterious
A3 Musician; bio-engineer
A4 Church; boy scouts; National Society of Professional Engineers;
UCSD A5 Professional Engineer; Fundamentals of Engineering

Five Sensory Descriptors
Look - happy and confident
Feel/move - firm; smooth; methodological gait
Smell - apple cinnamon; autumn
Taste - sour; salty; spicy
Sound - airy and harmonious

Eight Adventure Categories
1 Physical - golfer
2 Recreation - musician; pianist
3 Vocational - bio-engineer
4 Relational - married w/ 1 child; vacations in U.S. Virgin Islands
5 Financial - upper middle class
6 Educational - Ph. D. Bio-Engineering; Full Scholarship
7 Mental - skeptic
8 Spiritual - music ministry; missionary work in Africa

Character Translation Techniques Examples

Third, select images that represent the responses provided for the Character and World translation techniques.

Fourth, develop a two- to six-sentence Personal Mission Statement to add to the display with the images.

Fifth, develop a one word to one sentence Personal Conviction Mantra to add to the display with the images.

> Sam's World: Vision Board Part 2
>
> Environmental Factors
> 1 Atmosphere - electric; light; free flowing
> 2 Domicile - USA
> 3 Topography - Flat; sea level elevation
> 4 Neighborhood - Urban
> 5 Residence - Condo
> 6 Climate - humid: hot; non-snowy winters
>
> Five Sensory Descriptors
> Intrigues the eyes - vibrant earth-tone and natural colors
> Textures and movements - warm sea breeze; fluid and effortless Aromas - coffee beans and lavender
> Palette - sweet and sour; acidic
> Tunes - Classical music; grand piano and strings
>
> Personal Mission Statement (PMS)
> I am a purveyor of knowledge and follow the facts wherever they lead me. I fear no set-backs, detours, dead-ends or failures because each one brings me closer to the truth I seek. I work, play and love hard because I intentionally live life to the fullest.
>
> Personal Conviction Mantra (PCM)
> I know the truth and it sets me free

World Translation Techniques Examples

Vision Board

GAInS

First, review the Vision Board to determine which images you intend to make progress toward or accomplish during the given year.

Second, brainstorm GAInS Adventures you intend to accomplish during the year.

Third, draft a list of GAInS Adventures by category using the SMART Adventure setting method.

Fourth, input abbreviated GAInS Adventures into the GAInS.

GAInS Adventure List

SMART = SPECIFIC | MEASURABLE | ACHIEVABLE | RELEVANT | TIME-BOUND

- ☐ Join gym that has extended business hours, personal trainer and group training packages by 1 Feb.
- ☐ Reduce pant size from 36in to 34in waist by 1 Dec.
- ☐ Begin weekly lessons with a golf professional trainer by 1 June
- ☐ Try a new hairstyle that I haven't tried before by 21 Mar.
- ☐ Write and produce two original songs including instrumental and vocal arrangements by 1 Sep.
- ☐ Learn to play the bass guitar part for 3 songs without mistakes by 31 Dec.
- ☐ Complete the NCEES FE Other Disciplines Study Guide by 1 Oct.
- ☐ Pass the FE exam by 31 Dec.
- ☐ Take trip to U.S. Virgin Islands with at least one friend by 31 Dec.
- ☐ Increase credit score by 100 points using strategies that include reducing consumer CC debt by 31 Dec.
- ☐ Save a minimum of $15K in savings and/or brokerage account funds by 31 Dec.
- ☐ Submit application UC San Diego bio-engineering Ph.D. program by 1 Feb.
- ☐ Read 4 books about Greek Skepticism by 31 Dec.
- ☐ Invite a total of six people to attend Bible study with church fellowship by 31 Dec.
- ☐ Write and share a weekly devotional with others beginning by 1 Sep.

STAGE 02 — POISE GAME

GAInS Adventure List Example

T2D List

First, review the Vision Board and GAInS to determine which images you intend to make progress toward or accomplish during the given year.

Second, brainstorm which custom or generic E2As from the E2A List you intend to accomplish during the day, month, week or quarter.

Third, draft a list of generic and custom E2As to

complete during the predetermined timeframe. You can create new custom E2As, if necessary.

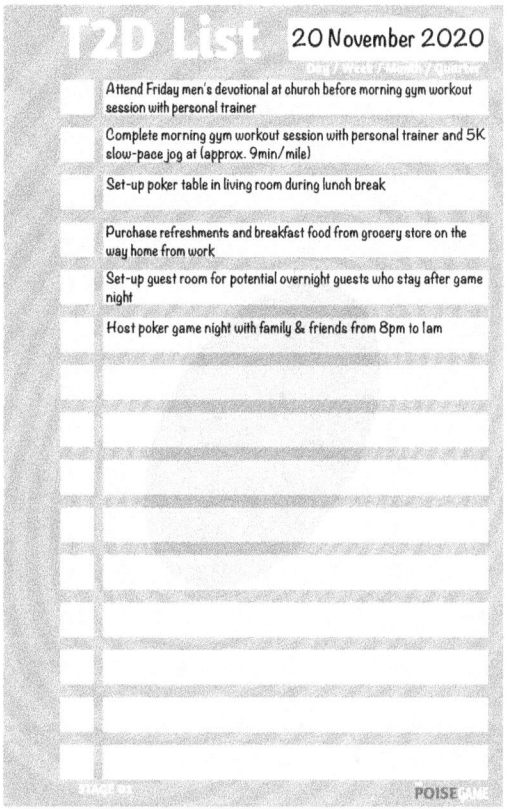

T2D List Example

E2A List

First, review the Vision Board and GAInS to determine which images you intend to make progress toward or accomplish during the given year.

Second, brainstorm E2As you intend to accomplish during the year.

Third, draft a list of generic and custom E2As by Vision Board image and GAInS Adventures using the SMART Adventure setting method for the custom E2As and the modified SMART method for the generic E2As.

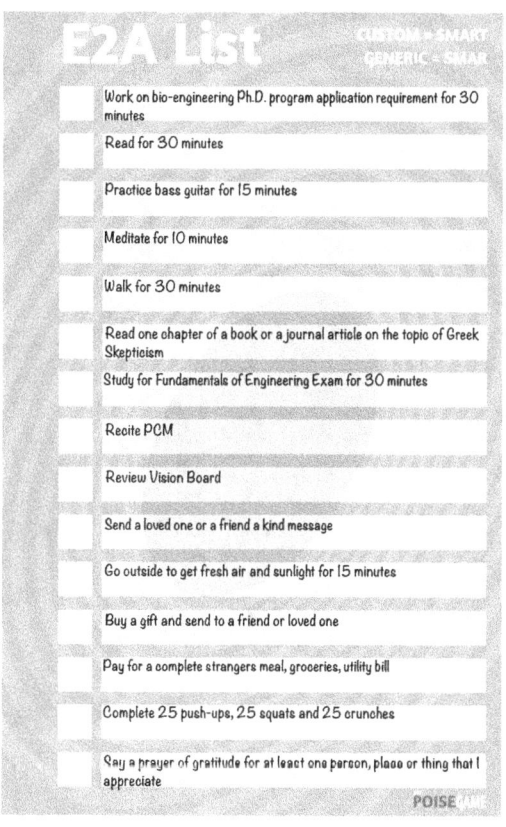

E2A) List Example

Poise Deck

First, review the Vision Board and GAInS to determine which images you intend to make progress toward or accomplish during the given year.

Second, brainstorm which generic E2As from the E2A List you intend to accomplish during the day, month, week or quarter.

Third, input the generic E2As onto playing cards. You can create new generic E2As, if necessary.

Poise Deck Example

You can also shorten the deck or input duplicate versions of the same E2A on cards, as desired. custom E2As and the modified SMART method for the generic E2As.

Poise Aspirant Dashboard

To create the Poise Aspirant Dashboard, download the Poise Aspirant Dashboard template from www.poisegame.com.

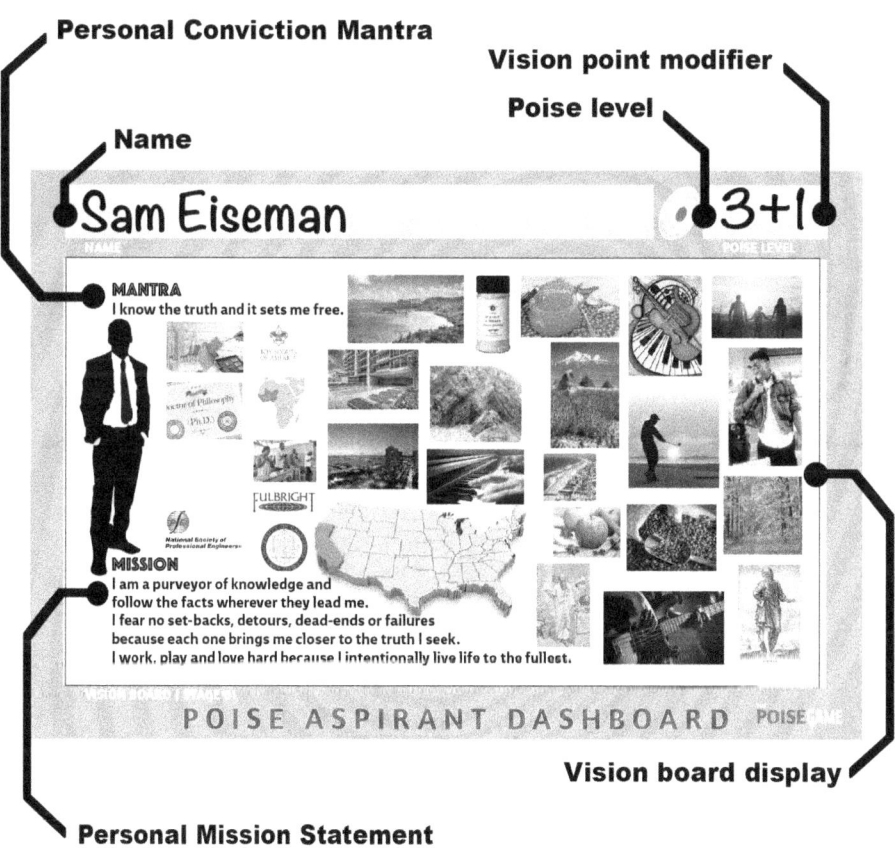

Vision Board | Front Side

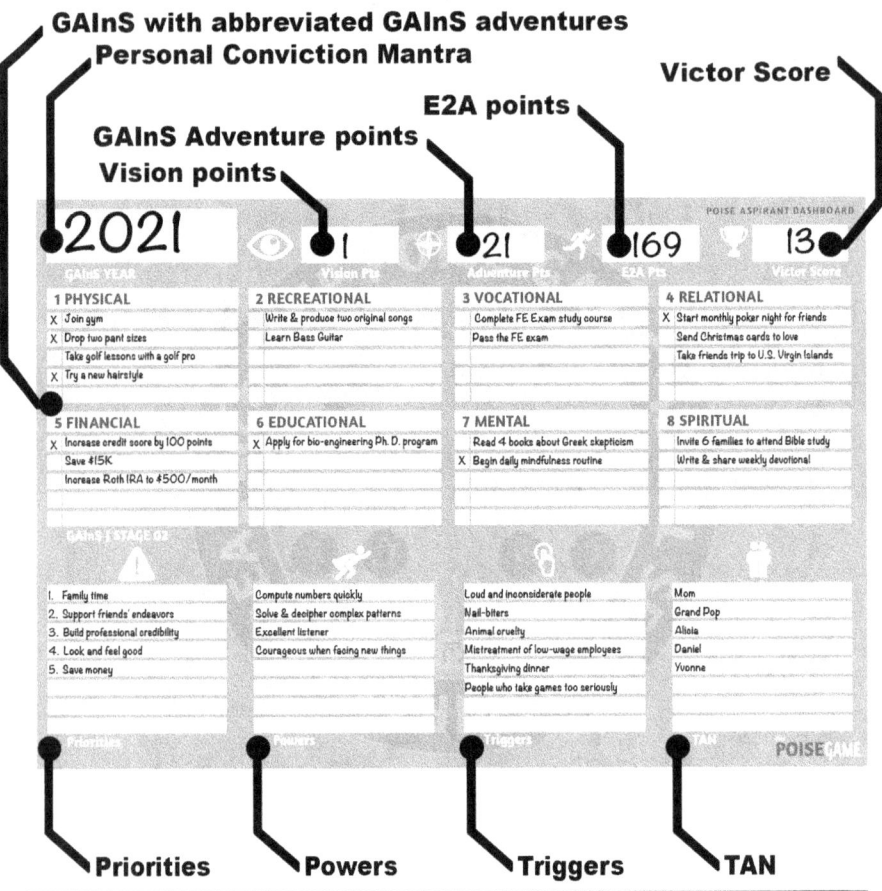

Vision Board | Back Side

First, write your name.
Second, emplace your Vision Board.
Third, input your GAInS year.
Fourth, input your GAInS Adventures.
Fifth, brainstorm and input your priorities for the year.

Sixth, brainstorm and input your notable powers for the year.

Seventh, brainstorm and input your notable triggers for the year.

Eighth, brainstorm and input your TAN members for the year.

Free templates can be downloaded at www.poisegame.com.

Glossary of Terms

Adventure Points – represents each completed GAInS Adventure. Adventure Points can carry over to the next year with the new Poise Aspirant Dashboard. If an Aspirant accumulates the requisite amount of adventure points, he or she can exchange them to advance to the next Poise Level based upon level-up guidelines.

apogee – an Aspirant's highest ideals. The manifestation of his or her best self and best life.

Aspirant – a person who has ambitions to achieve his or her highest ideals.

Be-Do-Have – also called the eternal triad, which an

Aspirant uses to assess and calibrate his or her conveyance faculties. Each component exists in harmony with the others and can generate the creative energies for the other component to be realized.

compromise – to weaken the integrity and functionality of a person's vision through the use of unproductive thoughts, emotions, words and deeds that are contrary to his or her highest ideals.

Four-pronged Conveyance Faculties – also known als conveyance faculties. An Aspirant's thoughts, emotions, words and deeds. A demonstration of his or her executive function of self-control.

d8 – the eight-sided dice that an Aspirant rolls to play stage two, GAInS, where the numbers of the dice corresponded with specific GAInS Adventure Categories: (1) Physical, (2) Recreational, (3) Vocational, (4) Relational, (5) Financial, (6) Educational, (7) Mental, and (8) Spiritual. Once the category is selected, the Aspirant can roll the dice to determine the GAInS Adventure within that category.

E2As – stands for efficient and effective activities,

which are custom or generic conveyance faculties that are productive because they align with an Aspirant's vision, GAInS and priorities.

E2A Points – represents each completed E2A. E2A Points are earned each time an Aspirant completes an E2A. E2A Points can carry over to the next year's Poise Aspirant Dashboard. If an Aspirant accumulates the requisite amount of E2A points, he or she can exchange them to advance to the next Poise Level based on level-up guidelines.

educational adventure – includes items such as degrees, schools attended, certifications, licenses, accreditations and other credentials.

Eight Adventure Attributes – used for developing the Aspirant's character traits for his or her vision board. Derived from the GAInS Adventure Categories, which include: (1) Physical, (2) Recreational, (3) Vocational, (4) Relational, (5) Financial, (6) Educational, (7) Mental, and (8) Spiritual.

Environmental Factors – includes characteristics relating to the physical space the Aspirant intends to occupy in your ideal state, which includes atmosphere, domicile, topography, neighborhood, residence and climate.

eternal triad – see Be-Do-Have.

expectations – a person's sense of entitlement that expresses his or her belief that he or she deserves to receive or experience a certain outcome because actions were taken that warrant it.

Farmer or the Fisherman Test – a two-question, check to determine whether it is appropriate for an Aspirant to have expectations or not. The farmer represents a person who should have expectations. The fisherman represents a person who should not.

financial adventure – includes items such as income, investments, retirement plan, credit worthiness, debt, royalties and intellectual property.

Five As – describes the Aspirant's character based upon five attributes including, aesthetics, attitudes, activities, affiliations and accomplishments.

Five Sensory Descriptors – uses five questions based on the Aspirant's five senses to solicit the descriptions of his or her ideal self.

Glossary of Terms

GAInS Adventure – one of the items listed in the GAInS Adventure Categories that is formed using the SMART Adventure-setting method. When an Aspirant completes one of these, he or she earns one Adventure Point.

GAInS Adventure Categories – adventure categories on the GAInS include (1) Physical, (2) Recreational, (3) Vocational, (4) Relational, (5) Financial, (6) Educational, (7) Mental, and (8) Spiritual.

Graduated Poise Pattern – the progressive approach to playing The Poise Game that is designed to develop your poise instincts and includes five steps: (1) Review, (2) Assess, (3) Refine, (4) Focus, and (5) Choose.

ideal life – the environment in which all conditions are perfectly suited to an Aspirant's desires.

ideal self – the fully-realized version of an Aspirant personifying exactly that which he or she envisioned him or herself to be.

Max Game-Mode – when the Aspirant plays the game as prescribed starting at stage one.

mental adventure – includes items such as philosophical practices and beliefs and worldview regarding human rights, economy, environment, politics, education, entertainment, justice and religion.

metacognition – Greek for "after" (meta) and "thought" (cognition), refers to the human capacity to be aware of and control one's own thoughts and internal mental processes.

Personal Conviction Mantra – a short saying, one word, a few words or an entire sentence, that an Aspirant can use as a deliberate trigger to focus his or her thoughts, emotions, words and deeds on his or her vision.

Personal Mission Statement – also written as PMS. A short paragraph, between two to six sentences, that highlights an Aspirant's visionary mandate for him or herself and his or her life.

Poise Level – an Aspirant's current level in The Poise Game.

physical adventure – includes items such as aesthetics, functionality and health.

poise – also known as self-control, a virtue that demonstrates a person's ability to self-regulate.

Poise Aspirant Dashboard – a control panel display featuring the Aspirant that comprises the tools and additional information in a single place for quick reference to facilitate his or her gameplay. The items that can be found on the dashboard include Vision Board with PMS and PCM, Poise Level, GAInS, Vision Points, Adventure Points, E2A Points, Victor Score, Priorities, Powers, Triggers and TAN.

Poise Deck – the card-based implement of The Poise Game that consists of generic E2As to enable an Aspirant to make choices that progress him or her along the path to his or her vision.

powers – abilities, skills and talents an Aspirant employs to complete E2As and make progress toward your vision.

priorities – a list composed of approximately 10 of the most important people, places, things, causes and ideas to an Aspirant. The items on the list are determined by the Aspirant and contribute toward his or her vision.

recreational adventure – includes items such as hobbies, extracurricular activities, social affiliations and any interests not specifically addressed in the other categories.

relational adventure – includes items such

as relationship status, parental status and preferences for social interactions.

SMART Adventure-setting method – format for developing GAInS Adventures that state adventures must be specific, measurable, achievable, relevant and time-based.

spiritual adventure – includes items such as faith practices and beliefs and worldview regarding human rights, economy, environment, politics, education, entertainment, justice and religion.

TAN – stands for Trusted Accountability Network, people who an Aspirant trusts and who have the Aspirant's best interests at heart. These people keep the Aspirant accountable to his or her declarations, values and vision.

T2D List – list of custom and generic E2As that lead to the accomplishment of Vision Board images, GAInS Adventures and priorities.

translation techniques – approaches designed to transfer internal images from an Aspirant's mind into the physical plane so that he or she and others can see it. The Character Translation Techniques include the Five A's, Five Sensory Descriptors, and Eight Adventure Categories.

The World Translation Techniques include the Five Sensory Descriptors and Environmental Factors.

triggers – situations that initiate unconscious and involuntary responses by an Aspirant that may lead to counterproductive choices, thoughts, emotions, words and deeds.

value – an Aspirant's energy, time, space and resources.

Victim of Circumstance – a person who limits the range of options within his or her perceptual field, then assigns responsibility for making choices to another person, the environment or the cosmos, even if the choice is contrary to his or her vision.

Victor of Choice – an Aspirant who acknowledges the range of options within his or her perceptual field, then confidently and deliberately chooses those which align most with his or her vision.

vision – mental pictures that represent what has happened, is happening, and what is to come.

Vision Board – a physical or digital display of images that presents the vision of an Aspirant's ideal self and ideal life. It includes the Personal Mission Statement and the Personal Conviction

Mantra. Stage one of The Poise Game.

Vision Points – represents each completed image on the Vision Board. Previous years' Vision Points are reflected in the Poise Level by adding a plus (+) sign and then the number of Vision Points accumulated. Current year's Vision Points remain in the Vision Points section of the Poise Aspirant Dashboard until year's end.

Victor Score – represents the count of productive choices an Aspirant has made despite encountering difficult circumstances. An Aspirant can add a point to his or her Victor Score whenever he or she overcomes a desire to think, emote, speak or act unproductively and choose to make a productive choice.

vocational adventure – comprise items such as your career, any additional occupations, entrepreneurial interests, business ownership and leadership positions.

About the Author

Joseph Payton helps people discover, plan, pursue, and achieve their life's purpose.

As a career military officer, certified fitness trainer and expert communicator, he's developed skills to effectively employ methods to achieve self-regulated, partner supported, behavioral modification in himself and others by combining lessons from several modalities, including psychology, rhetoric, neuroscience, linguistics, marketing, physiology and theology.

For over a decade he's successfully shared his tools and methods with people from diverse backgrounds.

He is currently pursuing a doctoral degree in Applied Behavior Analysis from The Chicago School of Professional Psychology.

He holds a B.S. in Spanish from the United States Military Academy at West Point, New York, a M.A. in Management and Leadership from Liberty University, and a M.P.S. in Public Relations and Corporate Communications from Georgetown University.

Joseph is married to the Glam Ish Up YouTube channel's beauty and lifestyle guru, Jancy Payton. They are the proud parents of two beautiful children one on the way.

THE POISE GAME

Play to Become Your Best Self and to Live Your Best Life

Joseph Payton

Paega Life Publishing

Send your feedback, inquiries, comments and stories to

info@poisegame.com

Get your free downloadable templates by visiting us at

www.PoiseGame.com

www.ingramcontent.com/pod-product-compliance
Lightning Source LLC
Chambersburg PA
CBHW071805080526
44589CB00012B/701